Beyond Rosemary, Basil, and Thyme

Beyond Rosemary, Basil, and Thyme

Unusual, Interesting, and Uncommon
Herbs to Enjoy

Theresa Mieseler

Managing Editor: Katie Elzer-Peters
Copy Editor: Billie Brownell
Designer: Nathan Bauer

978-0-692-19046-3

Printed in the United States of America
This book is not intended as a substitute for the medical advice of physicians. The reader should regularly consult a physician in matters relating to his/her health and particularly with respect to any symptoms that may require diagnosis or medical attention.

Cover Photo: Mrihani Basil, *Ocimum basilicum*

To Jim:
My husband, my constant source of strength and encouragement.

In loving memory of my Mom and Dad:
If only you were here so I could thank you for your encouragement in life
and for teaching me to respect and appreciate the land.

On Moss

Blessed be the moss that beards the face
of exposed embankments deep in the forest,

that spreads its feathery caul over old stones,
breaking them down, starting them on their way

from loneliness toward the community of soil.
And blessed be the moss that lays its carpet across

the north-facing toes of white birch trees, showing
the direction down paths where it will never go.

And blessed be the moss that comforts
the torn hoof of the starving doe in winter,

and that waits patiently, even beneath
ice-crusted, knee-deep late January snow,

to keep for us, who might otherwise despair,
the jewel-green promise of our renewal.

–Richard Broderick

Acknowledgments

This book is about herbs that are unique or uncommon. It is about plants that can't readily be found, and it's why people came to visit Shady Acres Herb Farm—because we had them. As I wrote about the herbs for this book, I learned more about their history, long-ago uses, and where they originated. As I created a list of herbs, I also realized I know some of the people who were involved with their discovery. Some, I didn't know, but I've always found people are willing to share their knowledge. There were people, plant connections, and stories to be told. It is these people whom I want to credit for their assistance and willingness to share. All the plants you will read about are ones I have grown throughout the years in my garden or on my deck and were ones that were available at the farm. Recently I grew them again, recorded data, and photographed each one for this book.

I want to express my sincere gratitude to all the people that were so helpful in writing this book. When my husband, Jim, and I first started our farm in 1977, we traveled east to visit established herb farms. Along the way we met and visited with Adelma Simmons, Gertrude Foster, Lynn and Peter Hartman, and Sal Gilbertie. They willingly shared their experiences. We absorbed it like a sponge, came home, and proceeded to grow our business. Some years later, other people who were influential in our lives were Kathy Schlosser, Don Haynie, Tom Hanlon, Jim Long, Josh Young, Chuck Voigt, Betsy Williams, Dr. Arthur Tucker, Pat Gould, and Madalene Hill.

The Herb Society of America and the International Herb Association bind many people together. The following are friends whom I have known through one or both organizations. Susan Betz and Pat Crocker have been inspirations to me throughout the years. We live miles apart, so we don't see one another on a day-to-day basis, but we are always connected via phone, email, and text. We chat about what we do and what we are going to do. Pat gave me recipes to use, and she edited all of the book's recipes. Pat knows her foods and herbs! Susan generously gave her lemon potpourri recipe; I call her the Queen of Potpourri. Thank you both so much for always being there and sharing your knowledge in this book. A friend for many years is

Rex Talbert—my go-to for nomenclature and botanical herb information. Thank you to Rex for editing the plant information on many of the plants, and I thank him tremendously for his ongoing advice.

Thanks to Susan Belsinger, cook and author, for the use of her basil recipe. Dr. Arthur Tucker was there with his expertise on herbs, nomenclature, and the chemical makeup of the plants. Chuck Voigt, the horseradish specialist, and Dorothy Bonitz for sending seeds and plants—I do appreciate it all. Exchanging seeds and plants with friends is a great way to learn about new plants. When I needed Hilltop Herb Farm oregano plants, Henry Flowers came to my rescue and mailed four beautiful plants to me.

I came to know many other plant specialists: Adam Arseniuk, for his research on tropical plants; Barry Yinger, for his discovery of *Angelica gigas*; Brett Jestrow, for sharing the story of *Nashia*; and Robin Middleton in England, for providing *Salvia* expertise.

Hassan and Susan Kaakani, friends from nearby, flowed with information about za'atar. Permission to use several recipes from Marge Clark's book *The Best of Thymes* came from a telephone conversation with Dick Clark. I am privileged to have known Marge, and Dick was gracious in his permission to use her recipes.

Herb growers made contributions as well. Richo Cech opened my mind to new basil varieties that have been introduced over the past several years, and his writing on these plants is very credible. Cy and Louise Hyde introduced herbs to the trade that have influenced many gardeners with new plants to grow. Conrad Richter and his one-of-a-kind SeedZoo™ offers many unusual herbs, flowers, and vegetables that you won't find elsewhere. Martina Slater, herb grower in the southwest part of England, readily answered my questions on 'Foxley' thyme and gave its history of development. When I didn't know the identity of an oregano, I searched and made contact with Rodo and Nikos Vasilaki, commercial tea makers in Crete who identified this dwarf oregano. It was such a pleasure to communicate with them and learn about the herbs they collect and use in their tea company. Peggy Cornett, Director of the Thomas Jefferson Center for Historic Plants at Monticello, was a tremendous help with the caracalla plant. It is unbelievable that so many people were so generous to share their stories. I thank each one of them.

Then there are the artisans who are so skilled at their craft. Patty Kenny is an expert lavender wandmaker. Her instructions are perfect! Kathleen Gips knows her tussie mussies, and her steps will guide you along the way. Thank you to both of them.

Kathy Allen is the librarian at the Andersen Horticultural Library at the Minnesota Landscape Arboretum. Kathy has been a great inspiration along the way, and I thank her for assisting with research and editing the manuscript. It meant so much for me to have someone with her expertise edit the text. Don't miss Kathy's writing about hibiscus and read her experience firsthand. Katie Elzer-Peters of The Garden of Words was willing from the start to help me self-publish this book. After sending a sample of the pages to Katie in late winter, she said "Yes, I would like to work on the book." Thank you for guidance along every step of the way and for getting this project on track. I also appreciate the assistance of the Carver County Library for their many resources.

My gratitude goes to Kristen Macauley who helped photograph several plants with which I had a dilemma; they didn't pose correctly for me, I suppose. Thank you to my friend Bea Osborn, who has always been there to help proof text and handle the graphics layouts for Shady Acres Herb Farm catalogs and newsletters. Bea was there to take my photo for this book too. For thirty-nine years the staff at Shady Acres Herb Farm played a key part in my life in the business of herbs. There are many of you, from near and far, who were coworkers. You were my friends—and you still are. We were a huge family of workers, and I appreciate what you did to help make the business grow.

Lastly, and very importantly, is my gratitude to my husband, Jim. Herbs are a passion of ours and a way of life. It all began in 1977 when I suggested we build a greenhouse. My idea was to attach "something to our home," and Jim said "No, we need to build a greenhouse instead." He has always been there for support, endless energy, and has been my plant partner throughout the years. It could be the end of the day, I could be out of energy, and work still needed to be done. Jim would say, "Let's get it done" and we both finished the job. When the idea of a book came to me, I brought it up at the breakfast table. I presented my ideas and what I wanted to write about. Without any hesitation Jim said, "Just do it," and that was that. That is the way it has always been, and I am forever grateful for Jim's support and love of life. We grew our herb business together, and he has been my equal in it. There were different facets where we each had our specialty, and we made it work together. I could never have had the experiences with herbs to write this book without Jim.

A view from Theresa's garden

Author's Note

In October 1969, I was in my last year of high school and one of my teachers announced a job opening at the Minnesota Landscape Arboretum. I didn't know what an arboretum was, but I thought I would apply. I was hired and worked recording plant data on weekends. All the plant names were in Latin, and I didn't have a clue what I was recording. After graduation I continued working full-time for several years in the office. I soon realized I yearned to be working outdoors, as many others were. In the mid 1970s Dr. Leon Snyder, the arboretum's director, said a greenhouse was to be built and asked me to run it. I was shocked and told him I didn't know anything about a greenhouse and his words were, "That's okay—you will learn." I took horticulture classes at the University of Minnesota, and I did learn through the help of mentors at the arboretum. A couple of years later Dr. Snyder came to me and said, "We are going to install an herb garden, and you will grow the herbs in the greenhouse for the garden." Again, I said I didn't even know what an herb was and again, he said, "That's okay—you will learn." After that I knew I could never again say I didn't know how to do something, for I knew, one way or another, I would learn. If only Dr. Snyder could know how instrumental he was in my life.

Herbs opened my eyes to a fascinating world. The idea came to my husband, Jim, and I to start a business, and in 1977 we founded our farm. We grew and sold herbs and educated people about them. Eventually we built eight greenhouses and expanded our business until 2016. The business included herbs and heirloom vegetable plants, a gift shop, plant mail order, classes and workshops, educational gardens, an herb fest, dinners, and fields of flowers. Where there used to be a swamp, there were gardens. Sales were at our farm in Chaska, Minnesota, at the Minneapolis Farmers' Market, and by mail order. We never used chemicals on the plants and our potting mix contained sterilized soil with peat moss and perlite. It made plants far easier to transplant into the garden with soil already in the mix, a practice rarely done these days.

Shady Acres Herb Farm was founded before herbs became popular, and our vision was never about just selling plants. Rather, we educated consumers about herbs, their growing requirements as well as their uses. We marketed freshly cut herbs. The class program at the farm was always popular, as we held workshops for container planting, cooking, crafts, aromatherapy, and herb gardening. That is what this book is about—sharing knowledge of some of the more uncommon and unusual herbs that have been around but which are not as well known as others. I hope the descriptions will make you want to grow some of them. I am so fortunate to be able to write this book and share this information with you.

Since the mid-1970s I have been learning, growing, and collecting herbs. Whether it's attending herb meetings, traveling, or visiting friends across the country, I'm constantly searching for a greenhouse or herb farm where I might find a new plant or two. Education and herbs go hand-in-hand, and that played a vital part in our business. People's desire to learn is always there. That is what is fascinating and fun about herbs—it is sharing. There is a growing interest in herbs, and our farm was a place of delight for people of all ages. My hope is that my book provides the inspiration to grow herbs that will be a delight for you too.

A strawberry jar is overflowing with rosemary

Round Top Festival Institute
Round Top, Texas

Table of Contents

Introduction

It's called "scent," it's called "aroma," it's called "fragrance"—it's whatever word you choose to call it. We are attracted to plants that have a scent, whether it be in a leaf, a flower, fruit, seed, or root. I grow plants for their fragrance, and that is what drew me to herbs. They are what brings me enjoyment. Many times, a fragrance, whether it's sweet-smelling or unpleasant, brings a memory or image of a time in the past. For me it happens time and time again. Azalea flowers in the spring remind me of my time at the Minnesota Landscape Arboretum, or the smell of crayons takes me back to elementary school, or cigar smoke reminds me of smelling my grandfather's cigar when I was eight years old. When I chop tomatoes, I remember my mom preparing tomatoes for canning when I was the young helper, and the aroma of dill takes me back to the kitchen, watching her as she made pickles. Even our local farmer, when he is in the field with his manure spreader, evokes a memory of time on the farm with my dad.

A honey bee is attracted to garlic chives.

But when it comes to smelling, there are times when you should sniff rather than take a deep breath, such as taking the lid off when making fresh horseradish in the food processor. I wanted to enjoy the fragrance and breathed deeply—not a good thing to do because it really takes your breath away. Recently, when Susan Betz created some potpourri, breathing in its fragrance took me back to a time when a friend was giving me a lesson on potpourri for the first time. As we all "mature," we don't realize that we are really collecting memories—all those scents are reminders of the past.

Herbs are useful plants for cooking, medicine, cosmetics, and fragrance. Think of lavender, rosemary, and thyme, all woody shrubs valued for their culinary uses. Old-fashioned roses, peonies, gardenias, bergamot, and scented geraniums are also grown primarily for their fragrance. A favorite of mine is lemon verbena; there is something about this plant that will cheer you or someone near you.

The herb garden draws pollinators, too, and they play a very important role in the garden. The bees, butterflies, hummingbirds, and even ants, are attracted to cat's whiskers, borage, sage, comfrey, lavender, mint, thyme, garlic chives, and basil. For most of us, these herbs are grown for their leaves, seeds, and flowers, but pollinators are just interested in the flowers. I've read in several resources that borage refills with nectar every two minutes. Perhaps that is why bees are constantly in the borage flowers.

Beyond Rosemary, Basil, and Thyme discusses herbal plants, uncommon or forgotten, that we enjoy for their flowers or foliage. Tropical plants featured in this book include Vietnamese gardenia, jasmine star, and caracalla, which are grown for their intoxicating flower fragrances. Grow them in pots and window boxes in northern climates or as garden specimens in the South. Plant herbs as garden plants in mixed beds or in traditional settings of symmetrical plantings or paths. Or, if you have a somewhat "wild area," plant reseeding herbs such as fennel, angelica, calendula, borage, dill, and lemon balm; they will provide a multitude of color with minimal work all season. Scatter other reseeding annual flowers in the area to add color and texture. Kitchen herbs conveniently planted near the house are easily accessible in order for you to snip sprigs of parsley, basil, or savory. Keep them close by and handy. For me, the deck is the best location where I can easily grow and cut the herbs I need for a recipe or meal preparation.

A garden near Raphine, Virginia

When winter comes around, collect nursery and seed catalogs. Begin your plan for next year's herbs and flowers with this book as a guide. Think of using herbs in the garden and container plantings for color, texture, fragrance, and for herbal delights for the kitchen.

The Met Cloisters, Fort Tryon Park, New York, New York

The Herbs

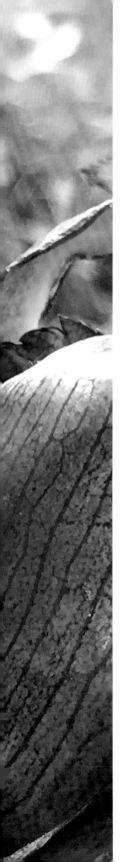

Angelica, Korean

Angelica gigas

Apiaceae

Angelica was discovered in 1917 by several plant explorers including Ernest Wilson. Just saying its name associates it with angels, and I have read that it was thought to have offered protection against witches. I'm not sure if there are witches in my gardens, but surely I am protected since I have many *Angelica* plants growing there. Korean angelica is native in Korea, Manchuria, and the Kyushu and Shikoku islands in Japan.

Description—Culture—Growing

Angelica gigas is an architecturally interesting and colorful herb that stands out among all plants in the garden. Unlike common *A. archangelica*, the showstopper Korean angelica is shorter and truly makes a statement of, "Here I am!" It is a biennial with large divided leaves that have a coarse texture, deeply cut with red veins, and thick with scapelike flowers that rise well above the foliage. The tight flowers appear during its second year after planting and are unusual in that they begin to swell, open, and unfurl, making it truly picturesque. The large purplish flowers are comprised of many tiny flowers that begin to open in early August. It takes up to a week or more for them to fully open. I always thought a time-lapse photography sequence of this would be spectacular. Bees, wasps, and flies are attracted to the flowers, and you will find them fluttering around the tops of the flowers. My gardens are adjacent to woodlands, and evidently the deer don't read the "No Trespassing" signs for most of my plants, but they don't touch this purple angelica or even the tall flowering

A. archangelica that also grows profusely. It prefers morning sun and afternoon shade in a somewhat gravelly location. I am surprised that more gardeners don't have this plant in their landscape because it thrives in northern climates—which can get down to minus 40 degrees F. Perhaps in southern parts of the country it will get taller, but the tallest I've seen it grow is five feet. It is also a minimal care plant.

Propagation

The easiest way to propagate Korean angelica is to let nature do its job. If you keep the flowers buds cut it is a perennial; if not, it is a biennial. Perhaps let one or two seedheads mature and keep the flower buds clipped from the rest. When spring arrives be sure not to disturb the soil around the original plant, and soon new seedlings will emerge. When you garden and observe plants you see how they propagate in nature, and with angelica, it certainly appears that seeds need a cold treatment to germinate. That is exactly what winter does for this plant. Once seedlings emerge they can be easily transplanted to other parts of the garden or shared with gardening friends. An alternative to the cold weather needed for germination is to stratify the seed. Mix fresh angelica seed with peat moss and store in a refrigerator for four to six weeks at approximately 40 degrees F. After this cold treatment, seed is sown in a soilless media in a warm temperature, 70 to 75 degrees F in a sunny window or under fluorescent lights, keeping the surface moist until germination. Transplant to small pots and plant into the garden when outdoor temperatures warm.

Uses

A. gigas is an extensively researched herb in Korea. According to many citations, in 2009 the research was being performed at the Department of Pharmacy, Kyungsung University, Busan, Korea. Korean traditional herbal medicine is widely used in Asian countries, including Korea, Japan, and China. Research has evaluated the importance of *A. gigas* and it contains several substances, one being coumarins. It has been used to treat anemia and as a sedative, among many other treatments. The study is available at http://www.koreascience.or.kr/article/ArticleFullRecord.jsp?cn=DDODB@_2009_v5n2_153.

Barry Yinger's Korean Angelica

Barry Yinger's first encounter with *A. gigas* was in August 1981 as the climax of a climb up Odae mountain that started as a day trip—but which eventually lasted three days. Barry was hosting a Japanese friend, Toshio, on his first trip to Korea before he returned to the United States after a two-year stay on Korea's west coast, and the two were accompanied on their climb by a Korean friend who was in transition from the Korean army to Seoul National University. They took a bus from Seoul to Odae as part of a short horticultural sightseeing tour. In Barry's words, "As my plant-appreciation circuits approached overload, I encountered my first specimen of *A. gigas* towering above the splendid chaos all around it. For a moment I was stunned, then suspicious. Not long before, in Japan, Toshio and I had discovered a patch of angelica with flowers of shocking fluorescent orange. After wasting a lot of film and emotional energy, we realized that someone on a surveying crew had neatly sprayed each inflorescence with orange marking paint. Could the mysterious angelica painter have followed us to Korea with purple paint? Fortunately, we found the mystery plant in *Illustrated Flora of Korea*. With the sad knowledge that the mercy of Buddha does not encompass those who dig rare plants near his temples, we finally moved, but I was determined to someday try to grow this outlandish perennial." Eventually Barry received a few seeds of the angelica, and they grew easily into husky plants and flowered in 1983. Today you will see *A. gigas* across the entire United States.

Balloon Plant

Gomphocarpus physocarpus

Apocynaceae

The balloon plant is known by several names including balloon cotton bush, cotton bush, swan plant, fuzzy balls, and wild cotton. It is native to open disturbed habitats in South Africa. It depends on pollination by insects for seed production. The primary pollinators are a variety of wasp species and, occasionally, honey bees. Seed of this interesting plant was given to me by my friend Dorothy Bonitz several years ago. I was fascinated by it. I learned that it is in the milkweed family and is often used as an ornamental plant. I first planted it by a fence line where it had support and also on the east side of a shed, but over the years, the plants have proven to grow well in full sun as well as afternoon shade. The genus name is derived from the Greek words *gomphos*, meaning "bolt or nail," and *karpos*, meaning "fruit." It is a unique plant to show gardening friends, especially when the balloons appear.

Description—Culture—Growing

An upright, herbaceous plant it can grow over six feet tall from its fibrous roots with a single main stem and many side branches higher up the stems. The leaves are mostly opposite, long, and narrowly oblong to lanceolate. The plant parts, flowers and leaves, exude a sticky milky latex that is regarded as poisonous if ingested. When the plant blooms, its small, waxy flowers with a slight vanilla scent are borne in the leaf axils. The petals are white to cream colored. When a wasp visits a flower, a leg or its mouthparts get trapped so the pollen attaches to the insect; when it visits another flower, it gets trapped again so the pollen detaches to pollinate the new flower. After it flowers the most fascinating part of this plant begins to appear: the balloonlike fruit. These fruits look like hairy, inflated spheres with pale green, soft, bladderlike follicles up to three inches in diameter covered with soft, hairlike spines. Plants are part of the milkweed family and contain cardiac glycosides, which are poisonous to humans, but the level of toxicity depends on the species and how it is prepared and eaten. According to the Ohio Agricultural Research and Development Center at Ohio State University, common milkweed is slightly toxic to humans, but only if it's eaten in large amounts. Milkweed poses the greatest danger to grazing animals, but there are reports that animals avoid it. There are studies that show when multiple plants are available, the animals eat everything else and avoid the milkweed. It attracts butterflies whose larvae feed on the latex and accumulate it in their bodies to deter predators.

Monarch butterfly larvae enjoying a balloon plant.

Propagation

Balloon plant is easily grown from seed, and once you have a plant you can collect and save your own seed for the next season. In Minnesota, the season is not long enough for the heads to open but they do mature, and I collect the silky seedheads. Sow seed indoors about six weeks before planting into the ground, after the last frost when the ground has warmed. Seeds germinate quickly in about two weeks.

Uses

These novel plants are interesting additions in the back of the garden bed or border as a single specimen plant. The fruits add interest and texture, and the flowers attract butterflies. I have used the stems in flower arrangements, and they hold up very well. The deer don't seem to bother this plant; perhaps they know about the milky sap it contains.

Dorothy Bonitz's Balloon Plant

"It was in 2015 in Southern California [when] I first saw this plant growing in a nursery. It had bloomed, and one pod had opened to show seeds. The nursery owner shared seeds when I asked if she had seed for sale. The best way to start is from seed from a friend who is willing to share. I use it in fresh and dried arrangements [but] with a word of caution: when pods dry, they burst and seeds can go all over the kitchen, garage, patio, or outdoors. I certainly recommend growing the balloon flower as a specimen plant in the garden—it really is a showstopper! It will reseed in my garden, zone 7, and it does not create a problem. It attains a height of four feet and grows two to three feet wide. Seeds are prolific and release easily from the pod. It is easy to grow, loves sun, and is drought tolerant. I recommend [growing] it in the garden for a novelty plant and everyone who sees it will want it."

Basil

Ocimum spp.

Lamiaceae

It would be hard to imagine not having basil planted in my herb garden. It is a tradition and a pleasure in the summer to cut fresh basil and to make pesto. The varieties are endless as well as the uses. Basil is a favorite of many because of the fragrance and flavor. They are native in areas of Asia, Africa, and Central and South America. Helen Darrah, writer and *Ocimum* specialist, writes, "Tradition holds that *O. basilicum* was introduced into Greece by Alexander the Great upon return from his Asia campaign. From Greece its cultivation ultimately spread throughout the world." Commercial production of basil is largely in southern France, South-Central Europe, and Southeast Asia. In Africa it is grown for its seed, leaves (for drying), and essential oils.

Description—Culture—Growing

The genus *Ocimum* comprises at least 65 species and some sources say it's more than 150 species. The main center of diversity appears to be in Africa. Most commercial varieties available are classified *O. basilicum* and include the most familiar types of basil. Basils are perennial but oftentimes they need to be replanted yearly in cold climates. I have seen one or two varieties reseed, and the following spring new plants emerge, but that is rare. Essential oils in the leaves include scents of lemon, cinnamon, camphor, and even clove. Dr. Arthur Tucker writes, "...the methyl chavicol provides a sweet taste similar to French tarragon, thus the name sweet basil, while the linalool provides a lavender-like floral odor." Many varieties of basil are showy ornamental plants in the garden too.

COPING WITH BASIL DISEASES

For most basil varieties, it may be necessary to soak the seeds, not for germination, but to disinfect the seed from diseases such as *Fusarium oxyporum* f. sp. *basilicum*, which attacks mature basil plants once they reach six to twelve inches in height. Affected plants wilt, eventually drop their leaves, and die. Since the disease can be transmitted through contaminated seeds, it may help to cleanse seeds by soaking for fifteen minutes in a 1:10 ratio of bleach to water solution. In this process you will notice the basil seeds swell with mucilage. Many basil seeds produce mucilage, which acts as a reservoir available for seed germination and early seedling development. It only takes minutes when seeds are immersed in water to produce the mucilage. One additional issue with *Ocimum* spp. is downy mildew, a rapidly growing disease caused by a pathogen, *Peronospora belbahrii*. The symptoms of this mildew on an infected plant resemble a nutrient deficiency such as nitrogen. Fluffy gray spores will be visible on the undersides of the leaves. Once basil plants become infected they need to be destroyed. This disease is difficult to control because it is airborne as well.

Propagation

Sow basil seed indoors about six weeks before transplanting into the garden, making sure all danger of frost has passed and the soil temperature has warmed before planting. Sow seeds in a soilless mix, cover lightly, water carefully, and place in a warm area; light is not essential at this point. Seedlings emerge quickly in three to seven days and need to be moved to a location where they'll get light. Transplant into three-inch pots and grow until you're ready to transplant into the garden. Basil is very sensitive to cold weather, and it is best to wait until soil temperatures warm to 50 degrees F. At that time, it's okay to plant basil in a well-drained soil in full sun. In cool-temperature areas basil is transplanted at the end of May.

Uses

Basil has many uses but the most common is for culinary purposes. It is used fresh to flavor vegetables, poultry, fish, salad dressings, and to make pesto, as well as to flavor jellies, honey, teas, and liquors. Basil can be used dried but fresh is preferred. Although the young flowers of basil are edible and can be used in salads and many other dishes, it is important to keep the blossoms cut off to maintain plant branching and to maintain fresh, new foliage growth. A favorite way to preserve sweet basil is to make pesto. I have found that drying sweet basil is not the optimal way to capture and preserve the essential oils of this plant. However, there is one basil that is excellent dried, and Mrihani basil is that exception. To preserve this basil, cut the branches and dry them in bunches in a low-humidity area for about ten to fourteen days. It dries beautifully and also can be made into pesto. For better flavor make pesto before flowering occurs.

Basils to Grow

GREEN PEPPER BASIL

O. selloi

Green pepper basil was first noticed around Chiapas, Mexico, near the Guatemalan border by botanist Dennis E. Breedlove, curator emeritus of the California Academy of Sciences, and it was later introduced to the trade. This area is also known for producing an array of edible plants including several varieties of chilhuacle peppers. Chilhuacle, which means "old chile" in Nahuatl (the language of the Aztecs), include three varieties: 'Negro', 'Rojo', and 'Amarillo'. These have robust flavors and are used to make mole sauce. Chilhuacle chiles should be roasted and peeled first as their outer skins can be a little tough. They all grow well in northern climates and produce a bountiful crop there too.

Green pepper basil is a tender perennial growing to about thirty inches tall with long, serrated, deep forest green leaves that smell like a cross between common basil and green bell peppers. Its flowers are pink with reddish bracts. It grows in sun and partial shade, well-drained soil, and, as a mountain species, is cold tolerant. I will admit it is not my favorite for culinary use but as an ornamental variety it is very showy and a novel plant to grow in a container with its serrated leaves and nice form.

MRIHANI BASIL

O. basilicum

In 2013 I was researching basils because the *O. basilicum* varieties that were on the market were prone to diseases. By chance I came across the name of a plant explorer, Richo Cech, of Williams, Oregon, who was collecting varieties of basil from southeast Africa, and the one I grew was the Mrihani basil. I conducted several unofficial experiments in my greenhouses. When downy mildew affected the 'Genovese' basil crop for the first time in my greenhouses, Mrihani basil was on the same growing bench—but not one Mrihani plant was infected. I moved a flat of Mrihani basil to another bench with plants infected with downy mildew; again, the Mrihani remained free from any mildew. I repeated the "test" several times until I believed (unofficially) that it is downy-mildew resistant, and I promoted it for this fact. I also decreased the incidence of downy mildew in my greenhouses by interspersing basil plants on benches separated by other herbs and using fans for better circulation. Spraying the basil was never an option in our business but preventative measures go a long way.

Mrihani has superb fragrance and flavor. It is a *must* in my garden each summer. The leaves are light green and ruffled, sometimes purple streaked, and it bears small lavender flowers. In the northern growing region of Minnesota, Mrihani flowers later in the summer, which gives more time for the plant to grow and produce foliage to cut and use. It has a sweet perfume quality with fennel undertones. Mrihani basil grows well in a window box or in a pot with other herbs.

Pasta with Summer Tomatoes and Basil

The great thing about this recipe is that you can prepare the whole thing in the time it takes to boil the water and cook the pasta—a quick, delicious summer dish you can count on. You can also use 1 pound of unfilled dried pasta such as ziti, shells, or bow ties, although the dish won't be quite as substantial as it is with filled pasta. As for basil, I recommend 'Genoa Green', a sweet green, spicy globe bush basil, Mrihani basil, or a combination of your favorite basils.

2 tablespoons extra-virgin olive oil, plus more for seasoning (optional)

1 sweet onion, such as 'Vidalia' or 'Walla Walla', diced

3 large, summer-ripe tomatoes, cored and diced

2 to 3 cloves garlic, peeled and finely minced

⅔ cup chopped fresh basil leaves

18 ounces fresh cheese-stuffed ravioli or tortellini, or pasta of your choice

Sea salt and freshly ground black pepper

Freshly grated Parmesan cheese

Basil leaves for garnish

1. Bring a large, nonreactive pot (such as glass or stainless steel) of salted water to a boil to cook the pasta.

2. In a large skillet, heat the oil over medium heat. Add the onion, stir, and sauté for 5 minutes until the onion is soft. Add the tomatoes and garlic and season with salt and pepper. Stir and cover.

3. Reduce the heat to medium low and cook for 5 minutes. Add the basil, stir, cover, and cook for 1 minute longer. Remove from the heat.

4. Cook the pasta according to package directions or until it is al dente. Drain, saving ¼ cup of the cooking water. Add the pasta and reserved pasta water to the basil mixture and toss well. Taste and season with the salt and pepper and a bit more olive, if desired.

5. Serve hot garnished with the Parmesan cheese and basil leaves.

Herbed Olive Oil Dip for Bread

Serve this highly flavored herbed oil with crusty French bread. It will keep refrigerated for several days.

1 cup tightly packed fresh basil leaves

⅔ cup walnuts or pine nuts

½ cup fresh parsley

¼ cup grated Parmesan cheese

2 cloves garlic, peeled and coarsely chopped

1 tablespoon fresh lemon juice

¼ teaspoon sea salt

1 cup extra-virgin olive oil, plus more if needed

1. In food processor, process the basil, walnuts or pine nuts, parsley, Parmesan cheese, garlic, lemon juice, and salt until the mixture is finely chopped. With the food processor still running, slowly pour the olive oil through the opening in the lid and process until mixture is well combined. Add more oil if mixture seems too thick.

2. Transfer the mixture to a jar, cover, and refrigerate. Keep refrigerated at all times except to serve. To serve, spoon a little oil onto small serving dishes, one for each guest. The guests will dip chunks of French or Italian bread in the oil—and they'll rave!

29

Basil

WELL-SWEEP MINIATURE PURPLE BASIL

O. basilicum 'Well-Sweep Miniature Purple'

If you have ever grown a small green bush basil, sometimes known as 'Spicy Globe' or 'Greek Mini' (*O. basilicum minimum*), and loved the shape, then you will love this purple-leaved mini basil from Well-Sweep Herb Farm. By the end of August, it measures twenty inches tall by eighteen inches wide. Its leaves are small, three-quarters inch by one-half inch. The top side of the leaves is a dark green with purple veins and the bottom is purple. It is a culinary basil with a spicy, sweet scent, and a slight hint of bitterness. The flowers in early September are pink-lavender. It is a showy plant that is perfect for containers.

Cy and Louise Hyde's Well–Sweep Miniature Purple Basil

Cy was inspired by a description of an obsolete small-leaved purple basil grown by Gertrude Foster, author, lecturer, and herb enthusiast. This treasure was developed at Well-Sweep Herb Farm in 1974 when Cy crossed a large-leaved purple basil with a tiny green-leaved miniature basil. Over a period of three to four years, more crosses were made, seeds were kept, and the offspring of each of these crosses were selected, resulting in a miniature basil with tiny purple leaves. To ensure the unique traits of this plant it is propagated only by cuttings.

BASIL, TULSI VARIETIES

Two of my favorite tulsi basils are Amrita basil, *Ocimum tenuiflorum*, and Vana tulsi, *O. gratissimum* basil. Although they are closely related to sweet basil, *O. basilicum*, the tulsi basils are used very differently. Amrita and Vana tulsi basil are known by several other common names but the most often used is tulsi basil, originating in Hindu. Asia and East Africa are home to the tulsi basil. Used in Ayurvedic medicine, tulsi is known as the "Queen of Herbs." A former name of tulsi basil is *O. sanctum*, which means holy basil. Many clinical studies have been performed on these basils, and they are recommended for a variety of disorders. To learn more about these studies, I recommend visiting The American Botanical Council website that has documents available, one notably in *HerbalGram*, Issue: 98 Pages: 1-6.

Richo Cech's Basils

Mrihani Basil

"Mrihani basil is a ruffled, very tasty culinary variety from the Pemba Island in Zanzibar, Africa, that I discovered. When I was there I asked a woman about collecting the seed. 'I want to collect these seeds and grow them out on my farm in Oregon and distribute them throughout the world. Is that OK with you?' She said, 'I give them with my heart.' Ever since I have been doing exactly this. It is also an ingredient in handmade perfumes or, as it is known locally, *manukato*, and is often worn in a small cloth bag around the neck. *Manukato* is the Swahili word for 'fragrance.' When someone uses an herb for *manukato* it means they are using it like incense or an essence. Mrihani is a common name in Swahili, meaning this particular type of wavy-leaved, licorice-scented basil."

Tulsi Amrita Basil

O. tenuiflorum

"Tulsi Amrita basil is a perennial tea basil originally from India. The plants are grown in isolation at our farm in Williams, Oregon, in order to produce the seed we offer. It's an outstanding variety for producing the true tropical-type tulsi tea (as opposed to the tea of *O. africanum*). Its leaves are green with purple highlights on a densely leaved bush. Amrita has a wonderful aroma and tests are very high for the eugenol marker compound and the anxiolytic compound rosmarinic acid. 'Amrita' is a Sanskrit word for 'immortality,' which is sometimes translated as 'nectar'—thus, 'nectar of immortality.' It tastes good and provides gentle stimulation to body, mind, and spirit. Growing tea basils brings many blessings to the household! This is the holy basil my wife and I grow for ourselves to make into tea. We find it very satisfying, with taste and aroma most appealing. Traditional Ayurveda usage is for stress, anxiety, heart disease, arthritis, diabetes, and dementia. Drinking tulsi tea in the morning is a fantastic way to start the day."

Tulsi Vana Basil

O. gratissimum

Known also as vana tulsi, clove basil, African basil, wild holy basil, and tree basil, tulsi vana is a perennial bush basil that grows to five feet. It's native to India and East Africa, a wild species brought into cultivation. Richo Cech writes, "These seeds grown at our farm are isolated from other basils. The plants are woody-stemmed and actually overwinter indoors more readily than the other tulsi types. I have brought them successfully through a winter, planted in gallon pots on an indoor windowsill. The plant is handsome and aromatic, slightly hairy, and green-leaved. As a garden-grown tea herb, it is a large producer of leaves, and may be used by itself or blended with leaves of other types of tulsi. Traditional Ayurveda usage is for stress, anxiety, heart disease, arthritis, diabetes, and dementia. The leaf color is light green."

Borage, White

Borago officinalis 'Alba'

Boraginaceae

Borage, known as the herb of courage, is an annual herb originating in Syria that has naturalized throughout the Mediterranean region as well as Asia Minor, Europe, North Africa, and South America. John Gerard, writing in *The Herball or Generall History of Plants* (1597), tells us that the attributes of *B. officinalis* were recorded as early as the first century AD when Pliny and Dioscorides observed that the plant parts added to wine made persons glad and merry. Dr. Varro E. Tyler, Ph.D., says these recommendations are still being repeated nearly 2,000 years later by modern herbalists. In medieval English kitchen gardens, borage leaves were grown to add to claret or cider for flavoring purposes. Interestingly, only tavern keepers, winemakers, cidermakers, and infirmaries grew borage on any scale.

Description—Culture—Growing

Borage is an annual with bright blue flowers and coarse hairy foliage. The white-flowering form is not as well known as the species, but it is even more attractive. When I first gardened with this plant I thought it would be a nice addition to the garden because of its white color. This is true, but I prefer growing it because it is a much sturdier plant and doesn't get leggy or tip over as its blue counterpart typically does. Bloom time is slightly longer, and when it reseeds in the garden, it doesn't take over as the blue borage does. It shares the same large, fuzzy, oval-shaped leaves that are grey-green and wrinkly. The stunning part is the lovely white flowers that are nicely star-shaped with their prominent black anthers, which form a cone in the center. The fruit consists of nutlets (seeds). It is a picturesque plant. When weeding the garden wear gloves when working around borage since the stiff, prickly hairs on its leaves can be irritating; it doesn't last long, but there's no need to itch. Borage provides plenty of pollen for bees, whether the flowers are blue or white.

Propagation

Borage is easy to grow just by sowing the seed in the ground. For a head start it can be sown indoors and transplanted—and it only takes a week to germinate. Once the seedlings are up and growing they really take off. If you're growing transplants, you'll usually sow seeds about two and one-half weeks before planting in the garden. Borage will reseed and fill in large spaces in the garden every year. Volunteer seedlings out of place can easily be removed with a hoe as they germinate; replant the seedlings or give to friends.

Uses

According to Andrew Van Hevlingen's article in the June/July 2006 issue of *Mother Earth Living*, he writes, "I first warn the consumer of the pesky little stiff hairs that protect this flower. You must bend the arching flower stems back carefully to reveal the flower, then pinch where the black anthers have come together to form a cone (known as a beauty mark in one herbal reference), while gently pulling away from the stem to separate the edible, star-shaped white corolla."

Traditionally, borage was cultivated for culinary and medicinal uses, although today commercial cultivation is mainly for the oil, which contains gamma-linolenic acid. This acid has shown use in regard to atopic eczema treatment, diabetes, inflammation, and possibly heart disease. It is not advised to eat raw borage seeds.

Cape Mallow

Anisodontea hypomandarum

Malvaceae

Cape mallow is a shrub or small tree in the mallow family originating from southern Africa. The name is from the Greek words *anisos*, meaning "unequal," and *odontion*, meaning "a little tooth."

The plants in the *Anisodontea* genus encompass approximately nineteen species. The plant leaves vary from lobed to, at times, no lobes, Leaves are alternate and the flowers are arranged in groups from the leaf axils or bracts. There are normally five petals that have deeply colored veins at the base. The petals will form a beautiful curved bloom facing up.

Description—Culture—Growing

This is an old-fashioned plant that once was very popular but is now rarely seen. It is difficult to understand why its popularity has declined because it is a pretty plant that blooms all summer. The entire plant has an attractive appearance, with a profusion of flowers from mid-May through September. This plant is very undemanding and only needs to be cut back before new growth begins in the spring. It thrives in full sun and can be placed outdoors in a sunny position during the summer, often attaining a height of twenty-eight inches. Plants prefer well-drained soil and regular applications of fertilizer. In freezing areas, overwinter indoors in a south-facing sunny window.

Propagation

If seed is available sow it indoors in late winter; it germinates at 55 to 65 degrees F. Typically, plants are propagated by cuttings that root easily in late February and March.

Uses

Plant it in gardens or grow in containers for constant summer flowers and enjoy the bees and butterflies that visit the cape mallow. They are very attractive on the patio or deck for the bountiful flowers they produce during the growing season.

Caracalla

Vigna caracalla

Fabaceae

The caracalla plant is valued for its highly scented ornamental flowers; I look forward to its flowering every year in my garden. Philip Miller's book *The Gardener's Dictionary* (1768) described it as "a kidney-bean with a twining stalk...(which) grows naturally in the Brazils, from whence the seeds were brought to Europe." Caracalla is native to Portugal.

The genus is named after Dominicus Vigna, professor of botany at the University of Pisa and director of the Pisa Botanic Garden, of the seventeenth century. The species name, *caracalla*, is a corruption of the Portuguese word *caracol*, meaning "snail or shell."

In correspondence in 1792 Thomas Jefferson wrote to Benjamin Hawkins stating, "The most beautiful bean in the world is the caracalla bean which, though in England a green-house plant, will grow in the open air in Virginia and Carolina. I never could get one of these in my life. They are worth your enquiry." Mr. Hawkins taught the Native Americans about agriculture during Jefferson's presidency and would receive plants from Jefferson. Perhaps

Jefferson first saw this plant in a greenhouse at Kew Gardens on a visit to England in 1786. By the early twentieth century, Liberty Hyde Bailey's *Cyclopedia* observed, "It is an old-fashioned glasshouse plant in cold climates but is now rarely seen."

Many years ago, caracalla was imported from South America and later was found growing in American gardens in the 1830s. Robert Buist, a Philadelphia plantsman, grew as many plants as he could at his nursery. He wrote in *The American Flower Garden Directory* that the caracalla was a very curious plant, with many flowers spirally twisted.

Monticello has had success in displaying and reintroducing this vine to gardeners. Caracalla is now more well-known and coveted by American gardeners than ever. In a phone conversation I had with Peggy Cornett, Monticello's Curator of Plants (Jefferson's Monticello, Charlottesville, Virginia), she said it is unsure whether Thomas Jefferson ever received seeds or plants of the species, and it has not been substantiated. Caracalla eventually was planted in Monticello's gardens in the late 1980s.

Description—Culture—Growing

Plant this vine in full sun to enjoy its immensely fragrant flowers when it begins to bloom. The delightful fragrance is similar to the fragrances of lilac, hyacinth, and jasmine. Caracalla belongs to the family Fabaceae (which includes peas, beans, lupines, and crown vetch) and is attractive in flower. The three- to five-inch coiled, shell-shaped blossoms are white and lilac-purple; older flowers are marked with yellow and cream. The flowers contain a special adaptation for pollination. When a bee alights on the lower petals, a leverlike action forces the stamens to protrude from a coiled floral tube, dusting the bee's head with pollen. Flowering begins in early August until frost on vines reaching ten to twelve feet. The nectar in the flowers attracts ants that will drink the nectar and spread pollen among the flowers, pollinating as they go. If the season is long enough the flowers are followed by slender, beanlike pods that contain several small brown seeds.

The plant is hardy from zones 9 through 11 and will die back in cooler regions when a freeze occurs. In cold regions in fall, cut the plant back and transplant into a large container leaving six inches of growth. When the temperature reaches 40 degrees F bring it indoors for the winter. In warm climates it is used in the landscape on a fence or trellis; in cooler climates it's used as a potted plant. It is a plant well worth showing off to your friends!

Propagation

Caracalla is grown from seed or cuttings. Be sure to obtain seed from reliable sources since I have had some strange seedlings grow from purchased seed. Soaking seeds overnight in warm water will speed germination. Sow seeds in a warm area and keep the soil mix damp until germination occurs. To take a cutting, snip three-inch cuttings in late winter after new growth emerges, dip into a rooting compound, and stick the cutting into a peat/perlite mixture in a small pot or cell-pack. Place a small plastic bag over the cuttings until they adapt, eventually removing the plastic. Usually it takes three weeks for cuttings to root. Then transplant into a four-inch pot using a potting soil mix.

Uses

This is a lovely plant to enjoy in the garden or planted in a container on the deck or patio for its wonderful fragrance and colorful blossoms. When it's grown in a container incorporate a trellis when the plants are inserted. As caracalla grows, wrap the stems around the trellis. In the garden use the same method of a trellis or fence. Plant in full sun. After planting the caracalla just sits there for the next month or so; it doesn't push out much growth. Then, all of a sudden, you'll look and it is out of control—it's time to fasten it to the trellis.

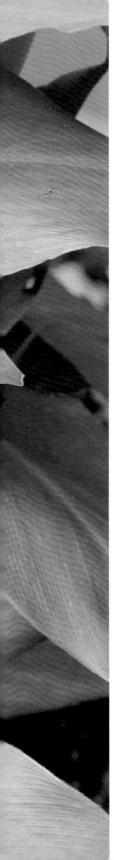

Cardamom

Elettaria cardamomum

Zingiberaceae

Cardamom is known as "Ilaichi" or "Elaichi" in India; the Western Ghats forest of the Malabar coast in India is the center of origin and diversity of cardamom. It is also called "Queen of Spices" and is native to southern India and Sri Lanka, where it grows abundantly in forests 2,500 to 5,000 feet above sea level where there is major cultivation. In world production of cardamom India is second compared to Guatemala, where it is grown on approximately 178,000 acres. In these areas the average rainfall is 150 inches. From 1990 to 2002 world production of cardamom was around 25,000 tons. Oscar Majus from Germany introduced cardamom growing to Guatemala in the early 1900s. It is interesting the history that often evolves around an herb, and such is the case with several spices including cardamom.

Spices have been with us for many years dating back to AD 1 to 250 and also from AD 1050 to 1500. It was during this time new evidence was found during excavations at the Red Sea coast of Egypt. The area is very dry and quantities of spices were preserved. In this area there was the small port called Quseir al-Qadim, which was a central transport center during the Roman and Islamic times. Several tropical spices were excavated from the site as well as black pepper, cardamom, turmeric, and ginger. In the past, spices were used in daily rituals, in the perfume industry, and for medicine. Later, the use of spices grew significantly in the Middle East and Europe. These spices were available only to the upper class of society. In pursuit of spices, people became entangled in altered social realities and political power struggles. The potency of spices went beyond their uses to stimulate the taste buds, delight the senses, and cure ailments.

Description—Culture—Growing

Cardamom is a perennial shrub in its native land, with large, fleshy roots and alternate, lance-shaped leaves, smooth and dark green above, pale, glaucous green, and finely silky beneath. Seeds constitute the spice element, and they retain their pleasant aroma and slightly pungent taste when kept within the capsules (fruits) that are harvested before they ripen. Harvesting occurs several times per year. The white and purple-veined flowers appear about five years after planting. When they're mature, seeds turn dark brown to black in color. A healthy plant averages about 2,000 fruits annually for market. Seeds are harvested, dried, and usually sold whole. As a cooking spice the darker seeds are removed from the seed coat and are ground in a powder. In India, Ceylon, and other places where it is native, plants grow to ten feet. Cardamom is one of the lesser known and less used spices we have.

In cooler regions grow a plant in a container and in temperate areas place it in the garden—it will do well in both spots.

Propagation

Plants in containers need to be brought indoors before it gets below freezing. In the spring cut it back, and new growth will soon emerge. It's a good idea to repot it at the same time—once a year is ample. When a plant gets big enough you can divide the rhizomes to increase the number of plants. Cardamom will thrive when it's grown in full sun or partial shade. Flowers and fruits will typically appear only when plants are grown under tropical conditions. Cardamom is a cross-pollinated crop and usually propagated both by seeds and suckers. Seed germination is often poor, irregular, and some seeds may even take more than one year to germinate.

Uses

Cardamom is used as a flavoring in three forms: whole seeds, decorticated (outer covering removed), and ground. Seeds are often combined with oils of orange, cinnamon, cloves, and caraway to flavor foods. Cardamom is traditionally used at holiday times in sweet breads and cakes. Seeds are added to the poaching liquid for fruit and also added to curries, rice, and vegetable dishes. Cardamom is an expensive ingredient, but few spices have such a complex bouquet that is floral,

An easy way to shell cardamom pods is to pound them using a small mortar until they split open to reveal the small pungent seeds.

smooth yet pungent, sweet, and warm. Following saffron and vanilla, the third most expensive spice is cardamom. Its production is similar to that of saffron and vanilla since it involves hand labor. All cultivation is manual, and the pickers harvest the pods with scissors followed by an extensive curing process. After harvesting, cardamom capsules are dried either in the sun or in an electric or fuel kiln.

Pat Crocker's Cardamom

"I love combining spices and herbs for flavoring all sorts of recipes, but I particularly love the citrus spike of lime [as well as the] hints of camphor and eucalyptus in cardamom. Whenever cardamom is used, it lends a warm and refreshing quality to food. Cardamom is thought to have [been] grown in the gardens of Babylon and, for me, the link to ancient people, gardens, and tastes is reinforced every time I pound the light green or tan pods and breathe in the exotic essence from [its] small, round seeds within. What follows is my version of a spice blend that can be used to flavor fish, chicken, vegetables, and grains."

Clockwise from top left: a spice wok (for roasting spices); a stainless steel mortar; a small cast iron mortar (with green cardamom pods); and a ceramic mortar

Indian Garam Masala

In Hindi, *masala* is the word for "spices." *Garam masala* is the blend of "hot spices" widely used in Indian, Nepalese, and other Asian cuisines. This combination is not spicy hot in my opinion, but you can always add cayenne pepper for heat. Many good-quality spice brands are now found in supermarkets, natural food stores, or Indian markets, but this is so easy to make. Almost all large, ethnically diverse urban centers have a few stores that sell dried whole spices in bulk. Until you know your consumption habits, purchase bulk spices in small amounts for making spice blends.

2 tablespoons green cardamom pods

1 tablespoon coriander seeds

2 teaspoons cumin seeds

2 teaspoons fennel seeds

2 teaspoons fenugreek seeds

1 teaspoon allspice berries

1 teaspoon black peppercorns

1 2-inch-long piece of stick cinnamon, crushed

1. Combine the cardamom, coriander, cumin, fennel, fenugreek, allspice, and peppercorns in a small cast iron pan or spice wok (see the Note). Toast over medium-low heat, stirring frequently, for 3 to 5 minutes or until the spices are fragrant and the smaller seeds begin to pop or jump. Watch carefully and remove from the heat before the spices begin to burn or smoke. Set aside to cool.

2. Using an electric grinder or a mortar and pestle, grind the spices to the texture you wish. Store the spice blend in a dark glass container in a cool place for up to 8 months.

Note: For roasting whole spice bark, pods, and seeds, a cast iron spice wok is ideal. You can find these at Indian spice emporiums or specialty food stores. You can also use a small cast iron or stainless steel skillet in place of a spice wok.

Garam Masala Chicken

A tasty dish that is quick and easy to make when you are in a hurry. It is full of flavor and the wonderful aroma of the Indian Garam Masala will tantalize the taste buds!

1 jar (15 ounces) green salsa

¼ cup smooth or chunky peanut butter (or another nut butter)

juice of 1 lime

1 tablespoon soy sauce

1 tablespoon Indian Garam Masala (recipe on page 47)

8 to 12 skinless, boneless chicken thighs

2 cups cooked rice (for serving)

½ cup chopped salted peanuts

2 tablespoons freshly chopped basil or parsley

1. Combine the salsa, peanut butter, lime juice, soy sauce, and Indian Garam Masala in a slow cooker. Add the chicken and stir to cover. Cook, covered, on low heat for 4 to 6 hours.

2. Serve with the cooked rice and garnish with the chopped peanuts and basil or parsley.

Cat's Whiskers

Orthosiphon aristatus

Lamiaceae

Orthosiphon aristatus, also known as Java tea, is native to Indonesia, Malaysia, the Philippines, Cambodia, Laos, Thailand, and Vietnam. It is now also grown in Southeast Asia, Africa, Russia, and Cuba. Dutch traders brought cat's whiskers to Europe in the late nineteenth century. On Java, an island that's part of Indonesia, there is a pleasant-tasting infusion that's made from O. *aristatus*, and in many countries it can be found under the name of Java tea or Javan tea. Plants occur in the wild in thickets, grasslands, along forest borders, and roadsides, often in shaded areas.

Description—Culture—Growing

Cat's whiskers is a perennial herb with square, stiff stems. Many times, two varieties are seen, a purplish- and a white-flowered form. The beautiful flowers are in terminal spikes held above bushy clumps of serrated, glossy, medium to deep green leaves. The delicate, tubular flowers have long, curved stamens that extend an inch or two past the petals, giving the long bloom spikes an attractive, whiskerlike appearance, which gave it the common name of cat's whiskers. In most areas, plants grow about two feet tall and bloom in late July until frost. In mild climates, they can shoot up to three to four feet and bloom through much of the growing season. This is an unusual plant that I highly recommend, and it is very attractive planted in groups and a novelty to grow. In northern climates it grows well in containers. In nature it grows in neutral to slightly alkaline soils in full sun. Trim it to keep it bushy and cut off the fading flowers to encourage formation of new flower buds.

Propagation

Plants are increased by stem cuttings, which root easily. Take cuttings approximately three inches long and stick them into a peat/perlite mix. With bottom heat they'll root within two weeks.

Uses

It is an attractive plant to grow for bees, butterflies, and hummingbirds. There is always a container on my deck with cat's whiskers and the flowers are extremely showy. In his book *The Green Pharmacy*, Dr. James Duke writes, "The leaves of this Java Tea (*O. aristatus*) are approved by Commission E for treating kidney stones. Make a tea with three to six teaspoons per cup of boiling water and drink it once a day. While it's not exactly clear how java tea works, the suspicion is that it helps open the ureters—the tubes leading from the kidneys to the bladder—allowing small stones to be passed." It is used medicinally in teas in the Philippines and Papua New Guinea as a strong diuretic against various kinds of illnesses. *O. aristatus* is one of the oldest and most popular herbal medicines in Southeast Asia.

Chervil

Anthriscus cerefolium

Apiaceae

Perhaps chervil was once a forgotten herb, but now, with so much interest in herbs, it can be appreciated that this delicately flavored herb deserves a place in the garden. It is sometimes known as gourmet parsley, French parsley, and salad chervil. It originated in the mountainous areas of east-central and southeastern Europe and Central Asia, and it has now naturalized in many parts of the United States. Although it was cultivated in Brazil in 1647, there is no mention of its use in America until a century later. It probably escaped from gardens where it had been planted and is now found growing wild in shady areas. Chervil is an ancient culinary herb that was used by the Greeks and Romans and was mentioned in the famous book *Naturalis Historia* by the Roman writer Pliny the Elder (AD 23–79).

Description—Culture—Growing

An annual, chervil loves shade. It will reseed and come back year after year. It emerges in cool spring weather, growing to twelve inches tall and sending up finely cut leaves that are golden-green with a sweet anise aroma and taste. The showy white flowers are arranged in umbels, which is typical in the parsley family. As chervil grows, pinch out the flower stalks as they form to prolong the harvest period; the flowers make the leaves less flavorful. It is also best to use chervil fresh because when you dry the leaves, they lose their flavor. You don't want to eat something that tastes like mown hay. When hot weather arrives, the flowers bolt, and pointy fruits are formed that ripen and turn black. These seeds will disperse ensuring a crop next season. At times it is confused with parsley, but the flavor is the key. Chervil is frequently referred to as gourmet parsley. Given the proper garden location, chervil is ready to harvest

six weeks from the time it is sown. It is short-lived when it's planted in a container. This herb is produced commercially in France and in the western United States. An interesting legend is that chervil makes one merry, sharpens a dull wit, prods the memory, and gives the aged the dash of youth—something to make note of!

Propagation

Its white taproot makes chervil plants nearly impossible to transplant when they are fully grown, so it is best to sow seed where they will grow. Sow seed in spring or early fall in a shaded area where the plants are to grow and cover lightly with soil. With ample moisture seeds will emerge within two weeks.

Uses

Chervil does not retain its anise flavor when it is dried, so when cooking with fresh chervil, only add it at the last minute. Gertrude Foster, who was an herb grower, author, and editor of the former *Herb Grower Magazine*, describes *fines herbes* as fresh herbs chopped or finely cut and added directly to a dish. The recipes vary slightly but may contain more or less a combination of fresh chervil, chives, parsley, and tarragon. A *fines herbes* blend is used in dishes containing eggs, butter, cream cheese, and sauces as well as in salads, tabbouleh, cottage cheese, peas, and fish. The mixture is added during the last few minutes of cooking or sprinkled (as on an omelet) just before serving. Chervil leaves can be finely cut and frozen in small plastic bags for winter use. In France, cooking with chervil is almost a requirement in home kitchens, restaurants, and hotels and is commonly used as a seasoning for soups. The dish sea bass with chervil (also containing red onions, mushrooms, and new potatoes) is another popular treat where people can easily taste the advantages of cooking with chervil. The sea bass is stuffed with chervil and served with a pesto over new potatoes. The dish is usually made only in spring, though it can be made later if you have chervil planted in a container.

Sea Bass with Chervil

Chervil adds a delicate anise flavor to fish but French tarragon is a good substitute if chervil is not available.

1 teaspoon extra-virgin olive oil plus more for oiling the pan

1 new red potato, cubed

1 teaspoon butter

2 tablespoons sherry vinegar

2 cups sliced portobello mushrooms

1 small red onion, sliced

Sea salt and freshly cracked black pepper to taste

2 fillets (4 ounces each) sea bass, cut three times diagonally on both sides

2 tablespoons chopped fresh chervil

1 teaspoon smoked paprika

Dash of hot red pepper flakes

To serve

2 tablespoons pesto sauce or Herbed Olive Oil Dip, see page 29

½ cup cherry tomatoes, quartered

2 tablespoons drained capers

1. Preheat the oven broiler and lightly oil a rimmed baking sheet.

2. Place the potato in a pot with enough water to cover, bring the water to a boil, and cook 10 minutes or until tender. Drain and rinse with cool water.

3. Melt the butter in a skillet over medium heat, add the vinegar, and sauté the mushrooms and onion for 6 minutes or until tender. Add the potato. Season with the salt and pepper.

4. Insert the chervil into the sea bass fillets, dividing equally.

5. In a small bowl, mix 1 teaspoon olive oil, the paprika, and the red pepper flakes. Rub this mixture on both sides of the sea bass fillets. Place the fillets on the prepared baking sheet and season all over with salt and pepper. Broil 5 to 6 minutes on each side, or until the fish turns opaque and flakes easily with a fork.

6. Divide the potato-mushroom-onion mixture evenly between two plates. Top each plate with a sea bass fillet and garnish with the pesto (or Herbed Olive Oil), cherry tomatoes, and capers.

53

Chervil

Chives, Ornamental

Allium senescens subsp. *glaucum*

Amaryllidaceae

The species A. *senescens* is native from central Europe to northern Asia (Siberia, Mongolia, China, and Korea). In its native area the species is found in dry, rocky places. A. *senescens* subsp. *glaucum* is a low-growing form that is grown for its lavender-pink flowers from late August into September. It is an ornamental variety and flowers later than the species. Plants offered under this name can vary in their color and degree of spiraling foliage.

Description—Culture—Growing

This compact *Allium* has silvery, twisted, horizontal leaves with a glaucous (bluish gray to gray-green) appearance. Because of this type of growth, it is sometimes called cowlick chives. This twisting habit becomes less pronounced as the season advances, but the gray-green leaves are enough to catch one's eye during the season. It is easily grown in dry to medium moisture in well-drained soil in full sun to part shade. At six to eight inches tall, it works well in a rock garden or in containers. On many occasions I have used it as a hedge in fairy gardens since it can easily be trimmed to fit the container. Rising well above the foliage, its small globe-shaped flowers are lavender-pink. In my gardens, I have it growing on the back side of my rock garden, and it maintains its shape well as the plant expands. When they were planted twenty years ago they were small, but the clumps have expanded to twenty-four inches in diameter. The beauty of this plant is that it I have not seen it reseed, as most other *Allium* species tend to do, when eventually you have a "chive lawn."

Even though the flowers are beautiful it is the unusual foliage that provides long-lasting interest in the garden. I've not seen any insect or disease problems and deer stay away. If the garden area is too wet you will see the foliage yellow, which is a sign to move it to a drier area.

Propagation

Plants divide very easily in early spring. I like to dig up a plant and hose the clump off with a spray of water—the soil washes away, which makes it easy to pull the roots apart to divide and replant. This ornamental onion makes a nice border around herb and perennial gardens and is so easy to plant once you have a couple of plants to divide. Simply replant to other parts of the garden and water well.

Uses

Its use is purely as a landscape plant. I know from experience that it is not a culinary *Allium* because I tasted it once—and I don't need to do that again. It does *not* have a pleasant flavor. It is useful in a knot garden because it keeps it shape for many years and has a great color contrast to other plants.

Comfrey

Symphytum spp.

Boraginaceae

'AXMINSTER GOLD' COMFREY

Symphytum uplandicum 'Axminster Gold'

'Axminster Gold' comfrey leaves are huge, growing to twenty inches long by eight inches wide. The leaves of the variegated type are elongated, green on the inside and edged in yellow on the outside margins. The plant grows as a bush forty-eight inches wide and twenty inches tall and does well in semi-shade in moist conditions; if there is a choice, afternoon shade is preferred. It is insect-free and holds up well during the growing season. Blue flowers form on the plants in summer months.

Symphytum officinale 'Well-Sweep Raspberry Queen'

The species *S. officinale* is native to Europe, western Siberia, and Asia Minor. It can be found growing in moist areas, along riverbanks, and at the edges of woods. 'Well-Sweep Raspberry Queen' comfrey is a perennial herb that grows to three feet tall and two feet wide with leaves that are twelve inches long by four inches wide. Flowers are produced in curling flower clusters. Its prickly leaves are larger at the base of the plant and become smaller toward the top of the plant. If you were to grow comfrey, this is the one to plant in the garden. After twenty years in my garden

it is still compact and doesn't take up much space at all because *it has not spread*. Plants begin flowering the first week of June and continue into early September. The one-half-inch-long flowers are a deep pink that fade to a lighter pink. With other varieties of comfrey, the flowers may fade to other colors such as pink, blue, and even white. I purchased it from Well-Sweep Herb Farm, and when I wrote to Louise Hyde recently, she wrote that it was a plant her husband, Cy, found growing in a field in Canada many years ago. This particular comfrey has boggled the minds of several growers in England as they were not familiar with it. Some think it might be a variety of *S. rubrum* and others, not. Whatever species it is, the bees don't care; they love it! It flowers from early June to late August and grows in full sun to partial shade.

Propagation

It is very easy to increase plants in spring before the plants emerge from the ground. Dig up the plant, wash the soil off the roots, and decide how many plants you would to replant. This method of propagation is by cutting the roots and dividing the plant. Root cuttings should be approximately four to five inches long and replanted about two inches below the surface of the soil. Replant in sun or partial shade in groups of three to five roots for a showier planting.

Uses

I recommend growing comfrey as an ornamental. If medicinal use is being sought please consult reliable sources. The following is used with permission from Steven Foster and James A. Duke from their book *A Field Guide to Medicinal Plants and Herbs*, third edition, 2014.

"**Warning**: Roots contain high levels of liver-toxic (cancer-causing) pyrrolizidine alkaloids. Certain types of leaf tea, although less carcinogenic than beer, were banned in Canada and elsewhere. In Germany, external use of the leaf is limited to four to six weeks each year. There is also a danger that the leaves of comfrey (*Symphytum*) may be confused with the first-year leaf rosettes of foxglove (*Digitalis*), with fatal results. Consult an expert on identification first."

Fennel, Bronze

Foeniculum vulgare 'Rubrum'

Apiaceae

Colorful bronze fennel is a licorice-flavored herb native to southern Europe. The genus *Foeniculum* was named by the Romans for the word *foenum*, which is translated as "hay." Fennel, along with St. John's Wort, was hung out on the Midsummer's Eve over doors to dispel evil spirits. If you have a need to do such a thing, hang these herbs on the door the night before the summer solstice!

Description—Culture—Growing

Bronze fennel is grown as a reseeding annual. This fennel's fine, feathery fronds are reddish yet slightly blue, which adds a colorful plant in the garden next to green herbs and shrubs. It may seem a bit strange but I have planted it in fairy gardens for a backdrop; it is easily trimmed and keeps its shape well in small, even tiny, gardens. Plant bronze fennel in a mass planting of eight to ten plants for a showy effect to display its color. An added bonus is that it is a host for swallowtail butterfly larvae; I don't consider the larvae a pest, although I suppose some may. In fact, the larvae never seem to harm the plants very much at all. Just plant more to benefit this beautiful butterfly.

Bronze fennel is used in the same recipes as other fennels, but it has more interesting foliage. I like to plant it in the middle or toward the back of the garden because in the northern climates in full sun it will grow to four to five feet. In spring give it extra time because seedlings from the previous year's plants will almost always emerge several weeks after the soil has warmed. Fennel stems are hollow with an anise flavor and scent. When you bite into a fennel seed the licorice flavor is from the volatile oil *antehole*, the same compound that gives anise its licorice-like flavor.

Propagation

Although it's a sun-loving perennial, bronze fennel is grown as an annual in northern climates. Fennel seeds will germinate quickly if soaked in water overnight (or at least ten hours). After soaking, drain on paper towels, and let the seed dry slightly. Sow outdoors where you want them to grow. Or sow indoors; it takes a little time to transplant the tiny, thin seedlings but it is well worth it. When bronze fennel begins to flower, cut its blossoms to maintain leaf and stem production (although this can be hard to do since they are very showy). Leave some flowers so you'll be able to harvest the seeds.

Uses

As a child, I remember my grandfather and father making pork sausage. I don't recall the exact ingredients, but I do remember they added fennel seed along with other spices to the long rolls of sausage that came out of the hand-cranked stuffing machine. That sausage was the best I've had, and I remember it so well. In Italy, fennel is highly regarded, and Italy's national liqueur, sambuca, is flavored with fennel. In England, fennel is used in soups; Germans put it in breads and fish dishes; Spainards use fennel seed to flavor cakes; and Scandinavians use fennel seed on rye breads. Fennel seed is also found in the Moroccan spice blend *ras-el-hanout* and in Middle Eastern *dukkah*.

Another use for fennel seed is in pickled beets and sauerkraut, while fennel leaves are added to salads and salad dressings. The flavor blends well with many kinds of fish, especially salmon; in the summer place a layer or two of fresh stems in a rack under grilled fish. Seeds added to breads, cookies, and biscuits are always tasty treats.

I have found that fennel does not dry well nor keep its flavor when it's dried. A better way to preserve its flavor is to freeze chopped feathery fronds in olive oil. Seeds can be air-dried on paper towels on a cookie sheet but note that, invariably, small insects scatter when you spread the seeds on the sheets; washing the seeds first helps alleviate this issue. From Dr. James Duke, the author of *The Green Pharmacy Guide to Healing Foods*, "I have often thought of the celery family as a stomach-settling family, and fennel, celery, and coriander are outstanding carminatives in this group. It could also improve the ride home for those prone to motion sickness. You can chew up to twenty raw seeds, just the way they come in Indian restaurants, to settle the stomach. In addition to a strong supporting cast of phytochemical players, (I won't name them all), fennel also contains the camphor."

Pork Patties with Fennel

Pork patties are easy to make and are a great addition to any meal. It's hard to beat these homemade delights.

2 tablespoons extra-virgin olive oil, divided

1 small fennel bulb, chopped; about ½ cup

1 pound ground pork

3 cloves garlic, peeled and finely chopped

2 teaspoons chopped fresh thyme

1 tablespoon toasted fennel seeds

1 tablespoon white wine vinegar

1 teaspoon sea salt

1 teaspoon freshly ground black pepper

1. In a heavy skillet, heat 1 tablespoon of the olive oil over medium-high heat. Add the fennel and sauté for 10 minutes or until it begins to brown. Remove from the heat and set aside to cool.

2. In a medium-sized bowl, combine the pork, garlic, thyme, fennel seeds, vinegar, salt, and pepper. Add the prepared fennel and stir to mix well. Measure the pork mixture and divide evenly to form four patties.

3. In a heavy skillet, heat the remaining tablespoon olive oil over medium-high heat or heat an outdoor grill to medium-high. Add the patties, cover, and cook 5 to 8 minutes. Flip and cook another 5 minutes, or until they're cooked through.

4. Serve hot on toasted buns or with crusty bread and a salad.

Gardenia, Vietnamese

Kailarsenia lineata

Rubiaceae

Southeast Asia, including Laos, Vietnam, and Thailand, is the home to this gardenia, which grows alongside streams in forests. The Latin name *Gardenia lineata* is a synonym for *Kailarsenia lineata* according to the website *theplantlist.org*. It has been difficult to find information for the Vietnamese gardenia, but it is well worth searching for a plant and growing it to experience the wonderful fragrance of its flowers.

Description—Culture—Growing

Vietnamese gardenia features beautiful white, solitary, pinwheel-shaped flowers that are two to three inches across. Not only are the flowers picturesque, but the buds, which are striped green and white before opening, are noteworthy too. The flowers have an intoxicating fragrance. It has two flowering periods—late April to early June and again mid-September into October. The leaves, four inches by two inches, are oval and semi-glossy with a smidge of puckering. It grows as an upright bush, two to three feet high, and is very attractive even without flowers, making it an ideal plant for containers. Full sun to partial shade is preferable for optimal growth. It prefers porous soil (good drainage) that's slightly acidic; that is why the use of a fertilizer for acid-loving plants is recommended. When the weather turns close to freezing, bring it indoors to a spot by a nice sunny window. Even though it may have a different botanical name, this garden favorite is still commonly referred to as a gardenia even though it now has the genus name of *Kailarsenia*.

Another common name is cape jasmine—but no matter what you call it, the fragrance of a *Kailarsenia* is unforgettable. Gardenias make good container plants and can be enjoyed indoors where they're not winter hardy. Be sure to prune after flowering. Place a pot or plant it near walks, patios, and within easy reach for sniffing.

Propagation

The only way I have propagated this plant is to take stem cuttings. The best time of year to take cuttings is in February or early March. With sharp pruning shears, remove tip cuttings from the stock plant. These cuttings preferably should be from softwood and three to four inches long. Dip the cuttings into a weak hormone powder that will help initiate root growth. Remove the lower two leaves before inserting into a container filled with a soilless mix. After inserting the lower three-quarters inch of the cutting into the mix, water well and place in a warm area, preferably with a bottom heat of 80 degrees F in bright light. For the next week keep the cutting partially covered with a plastic bag, cut on the sides for ventilation. After a week remove the plastic as it should not be needed. Generally, it will take four to six weeks for the cuttings to send out roots at which time the cuttings can be transplanted into a potting mixture. It is not uncommon to see gardenias turn yellow, especially when growing outdoors in the summer. This means they are lacking nitrogen and need a high nitrogen fertilizer.

Uses

Growing this plant is purely for pleasure as it is so spectacular on a patio or deck. When it's not in bloom, just sit back and wait for it to flower—and inhale deeply. It won't disappoint you.

Garlic Plant

Bignonia aequinoctialis

Bignoniaceae

The unique garlic plant is native to Mexico, Central America, and South America. In the Amazonian rainforest it is known as Ajos Sacha, Ajo Sacho, or Ajossacha, which all translate to "false garlic" in Spanish. The plant can also be found in gardens of Southeast Asia and other tropical regions, as well as a houseplant in temperate zones. Other English names by which it is known are garlic creeper, garlic shrub, garlic rope, and Amazonian garlic bush. The botanical name has changed, and the currently accepted name is *B. aequinoctialis*. Other Latin names it has been known as include *Cydista aequinoctialis*, *Adenocalymma alliaceum*, *Mansoa alliacea*, and *Pseudocalymma alliaceum*.

To the indigenous tribes of the Amazon basin, Ajos Sacha is an often used and well-respected plant. Most consider the plant to be magical or spiritual, capable of driving off evil spirits and bringing good luck. Bunches of leaves can often be found hanging in their homes for this purpose, and sometimes the leaves are burned over people or houses for the same purpose. John Miers first described the genus *Cydista* in 1863, based on *Bignonia aequinoctialis*. [Note: *Cydista* was its prior genus name.]

Description—Culture—Growing

Grown as a container plant in colder climates, garlic plant is a beautiful ornamental climber with leaves that smell of garlic when crushed. It is an evergreen semi-woody vine that can climb up to forty feet (in its native lands), but in our gardens it is usually around four to six feet. Leaves are bright green, four inches long and one inch wide. Tendrils aid the plant as it grows and attaches to a trellis or fence in full sun. In my northern climate, where it will not survive the winter, I keep in a large, fourteen-inch-wide container year-round. Move it outdoors, in full sun, when danger of frost has passed. In temperate zones it will cling to tree trunks, fences, or walls, and always needs a support to attach itself. It likes high temperatures and humidity, and if it falls below freezing, it will not survive. In order to produce flowers, garlic plant requires full sun. I've seen it abundant with flowers in a Minnesota garden with flowers lasting four weeks or more, changing from lavender to violet to almost white in color. All three colors can be found at the same time. To continue blooms cut off the old flowers and new buds will appear. Its garlicky aroma is released only when the leaves are crushed or pruned.

Propagation

Propagate this plant by cuttings in early spring. Each cutting should have at least three or four nodes with the bottom leaves removed. Dip cuttings into a weak rooting hormone and stick them into a mixture of peat and perlite. I admit that I have only procured a plant from a nursery and have not grown it from cuttings myself, but the grower assured me it was the best method of propagation

Uses

Ethnobotanical reports include the use of *Bignonia* branches for basket weaving in Mexico's Yucatan Peninsula, the incorporation of this plant into an infusion used as eye drops, and its use as an extract to treat skin ailments and ringworm. In the Amazon region local people use the leaves of garlic plant as a seasoning and spice. Fresh young leaves and stems can be chopped and used like chives to sprinkle on salads, sandwiches, and mashed potatoes. It is also well known and popular in the cities and towns in the Amazon and has a long history of being used in herbal medicine in Peru and Brazil. Both the bark and the leaves are used in tinctures and decoctions.

Hibiscus, Red Roselle of Rwanda

Hibiscus sabdariffa

Malvaceae

The origin of this hibiscus is somewhat obscure but it probably is from tropical Africa. It escaped cultivation and became naturalized in tropical America and Asia and now is cultivated throughout West Africa. It has been known by other names, too, such as rozelle, sorrel, red sorrel, Jamaica sorrel, Guinea sorrel, Queensland jelly plant, lemon bush, and Florida cranberry. Mathias de l'Obel, a Flemish physician and botanist, recorded his observations of roselle in 1576. Some years later in Java in 1687, it was recorded that its leaves were edible. Roselle was being cultivated for food use before 1840 in Guatemala. Currently roselle is attracting the attention of food and beverage manufacturers and pharmaceutical concerns for its possibilities as a natural food product and to replace the colorant in synthetic dyes.

In an experiment with chickens that consumed alcohol, the chickens became less inebriated after eating roselle extracts. Perhaps it is curious indeed that in Guatemala, roselle "ade" is a favorite remedy for hangovers.

Description—Culture—Growing

These fast-growing plants are frost-tender, require a well-drained soil, and prefer full sunlight. It is a showy annual shrub that grows to about four feet in height and almost as broad, with large, lobed, serrated reddish leaves and attractive, pale yellow flowers with a maroon center. The serrated leaves are about six inches across and deeply dissected into five narrow lobes. Stems, branches, leaf veins, and petioles

are all reddish purple. Roselle plants normally begin to flower after three months and continue for another six months. The flowers last only one day, and then red calyces form around the large seedpods which can be dried for tea-making or frozen for later use. In Florida, roselle is often planted in rows where it forms a dense hedge by late summer. I obtained my seed of *Hibiscus sabdariffa* from the SeedZoo™.

Propagation

Roselle plants are propagated either from seeds or cuttings. Seeds grow quickly; I once sowed seeds on April 14, they germinated on April 23, and I transplanted the seedlings two weeks later. During the summer the plant grew in a twelve-inch by twelve-inch by fifteen-inch container in full sun. It did very well, attaining a height of four feet by the end of the summer.

Uses

Hibiscus is used as a condiment to flavor meats and fish, as a natural food colorant, and as a sweet-sour addition to herbal teas. Another use is in the alcoholic and non-alcoholic drinks that are very popular in African and Latin American countries. Roselle's seeds are eaten roasted or ground into meal and, although tasting somewhat bitter, the meal is high in protein. Some consume the leaves, raw or cooked, with other vegetables, meat, and fish dishes. The flower petals are edible, too, and are added to salads and used as garnishes. Roselle juice is similar to cranberry juice, but it's not as bitter. In Africa, the leaves are frequently cooked as a side dish to be eaten with pulverized peanuts. Roselle sauce or syrup is often added to puddings, cake frosting, gelatins, and salad dressings; it's also poured over gingerbread, pancakes, waffles, and ice cream.

Kathy Allen's Hibiscus Red Roselle of Rwanda

"I moved to Malawi (Africa) in the 1980s to work at an agricultural research station for a year and ended up staying eight years. 'The Warm Heart of Africa' holds a special place in my heart—beautiful landscapes and warm, welcoming people. Recently I returned and caught up with some old friends who are now retired from the Bunda College of Agriculture. Analytical biochemist Dr. Timothy Ngwira turned his winemaking hobby into a family business named Linga Winery by using locally grown fruits. During my visit I was able to tour the winery and sample several types. My favorite was Rosella, a medium-sweet rosé made from the bright red fleshy sepals of chidede, or *Hibiscus sabdariffa*. The Linga Winery Facebook page describes Rosella as, 'A rich lingering rosé with sherry like overtones. The fruit is renowned for its cholesterol-reducing properties. A happy celebratory experience. The original and still one of the most popular Linga varieties. Sometimes used as Altar Wine.' Locals cook the calyces of this plant species (whose fruits are harvested March to May), [and] then add a little potash (to counter the acidity) and some crushed peanuts for a nutritious side dish. Occasionally the leaves are cooked in the same way. Europeans in Malawi use the calyces stewed with other fruit to sweeten the mix. According to *Useful Plants of Malawi* (Jessie Williamson, 1975 edition) roselle also makes very good jelly. While *H. sabdariffa* is cultivated in Malawi, several other hibiscus species are wild. [The] leaves and sometimes flowers of the wild species are cooked in the same manner, and a few are useful for fiber."

Rosella Rosé Wine

Author's Note: While perusing Richter's catalog I happened upon the SeedZoo™ and was amazed to learn of the many hard-to-find seeds that are available on this site. It is here where I found this hibiscus's seed and its history.

Conrad Richter, Richters Herbs SeedZoo™

"SeedZoo™ is a project to preserve traditional and indigenous food plants from around the world. Teaming up with botanical explorers and ethnobotanists, we search for rare and endangered food plants that home gardeners can grow and enjoy and help to preserve. Of the 7,000 or so species of food plants known to man, only 140 are cultivated commercially; of those, most of the world's supply of food depends on just twelve. Even as the world increasingly speaks about food security, incredible varieties that are known only to a single tribe or [that are located] in small and remote localities are being lost forever.

"We send plant explorers across the world in search of rare beans, squashes, melons, greens, and grains. They have been to the jungles of Borneo, to small farms in Japan and Italy, and to the bustling food markets of Africa. In the coming months they will visit India, Vietnam, and beyond. Many of the rare and exotic plants that they bring back don't even have names and can only be called landraces—plants with unique features that are found in only one region or, sometimes, in just one village. Often our explorers can bring back only a handful of seeds, sometimes fewer than one hundred. Because these seeds are so rare and from such remote regions of the world, they are sold on a 'first come, first served' basis. Once they sell out they may never be available again."

Visit www.richters.com/SeedZoo for a listing of the SeedZoo™ plants.

Horseradish, Variegated

Armoracia rusticana 'Variegata'

Brassicaceae

Horseradish is a hardy perennial native to the area of eastern Europe and western Asia from the Caspian Sea through Russia, and from Poland to Finland. Horseradish roots have been ground into a spice, prepared as a condiment, and used medicinally for more than 3,000 years. In the sixteenth century, Europeans began using horseradish for its medicinal applications. Another use was to infuse it in milk to clarify the skin and remove freckles. In England, it only became popular in the late 1600s and only then among the country people and strong laboring men as it was deemed "too strong for tender and gentle stomaches." But soon it became the standard accompaniment to beef and oysters. It was grown at inns and coach stations to make cordials for travelers. Its arrival in North America was from settlers who brought it early in the colonial period. It was common in the Northeast by 1806 and reported growing wild near Boston. In the present day, horseradish is still served as a popular condiment and sauce. In 2005, the Horseradish Information Council reported that in the United States, twenty-four million pounds of horseradish roots were processed into six million gallons of prepared horseradish sauce—that is a lot of horseradish! In the United States horseradish production takes place in Illinois in the Mississippi River Valley region and has since the 1890s. It is grown on about 1,500 acres with a yield of approximately four tons of roots per acre. Other large production areas include Eau Claire, Wisconsin, and Tule Lake, California.

Description—Culture—Growing

Horseradish is easy to grow in full sun and slightly moist soil. The variegated form of horseradish is striking with its white-and-green foliage, although the variegated form varies from plant to plant and some years has no variegation. The showy leaves can have large areas of white including some leaves that are completely white. But, usually, the large, undulating leaves are textured with splashes of cream and dark green. I call it the "queen of horseradish."

It grows in clumps radiating out from the main taproot. Small, white, four-petaled flowers grow from a stalk that can reach two to three feet tall when it's flowering (I keep the flowering stalks cut off). The young tender leaves can be harvested for use in salads but the main use is its root. To maintain healthy roots, it is best to dig and harvest the crop each fall; if this is not done, the roots tend to get woody. Even if you think you may have dug all of the horseradish, don't worry, because you didn't—and any little piece of root left in the ground will take hold and grow the following spring (for better or for worse). Horseradish contains minerals such as phosphorous, calcium, magnesium, and potassium. Horseradish is best when the roots are harvested in the fall after a hard frost.

Propagation

Roots should be planted in spring or fall so the top of the root, where the shoots emerge, is slightly below the soil level. Actually, I don't think it matters which way it is planted since I typically don't pay attention to root orientation, and it always comes up the following spring. After planting it requires little maintenance. If you can find the variegated form it is extremely colorful in the garden in spring, and it is worth acquiring. It seems as if the variegation might come more dependably if grown from a crown division, where the variegation already exists, rather from a root cutting, which has to develop adventitious buds. However, this has not been accredited nor have I tried this both ways.

Uses

Whether variegated or not, in cooking the term "prepared horseradish" refers to the grated root mixed with vinegar. It can also be prepared with heavy cream and is often served with roast beef, seafood, and on sandwiches. I love to add a small amount to Bloody Mary cocktails for an extra *zing*. The heat of horseradish is different from that of a hot pepper in that it is a quick heat—it comes and goes—rather than the lingering aftereffects of some peppers. You also do not acclimate to horseradish's heat the way people do to capsaicin, needing ever-larger amounts for the same zing; horseradish burns the same every time as it did the first time. In my family, we had a tradition of making horseradish where afterward we would have a brat and sauerkraut feast to celebrate. One time, my husband, Jim, decided to eat a whopping scoop of this freshly made recipe of horseradish. After consuming it he immediately left the table and broke into a sweat on the back of his neck; the intensity was so hot he couldn't talk for a few seconds! It's best to start out preparing small amounts and consuming it fresh, because as it ages it gets weaker in flavor. Always store prepared horseradish in the refrigerator.

Chuck Voigt's Horseradish

"Pungency of the horseradish mixture is controlled by timing the addition of vinegar to the ground product because the chemical process producing the pungency is halted and stabilized by vinegar. If you wait longer to add the vinegar, you'll end up with a more pungent product. A plant requires a long growing season to develop an acceptable root system. A continuous supply of nutrients and moisture is necessary for best leaf growth during the summer months. Most of the root enlargement occurs during the cooler temperatures of early fall. Locations in the northern half of the country, or in the higher elevations farther south, are better for high quality and yield. While horseradish is a long-lived perennial plant, for production of large, fleshy roots, it is most often treated as an annual crop. As it grows, its large roots produce small, secondary roots that are, in turn, used for planting stock the following year. In large commercial fields, horseradish is planted with the roots placed two feet apart in furrows thirty inches apart, with the crown end slightly elevated. Planted at this spacing, the number would be about 8,700 plants per acre! These root cuttings are covered with four to five inches of soil. Planting usually is done as early in spring as possible to maximize the growing season. In fall, when roots are harvested, digging must be deep to recover both the fully sized, usable root and the sets roots because the root system penetrates very deeply into the soil. Today most roots are harvested commercially with converted potato diggers that undercut, lift, and shake dirt from the roots. Home plantings will most likely have to hand-dug."

Collinsville, Illinois, known as the "Horseradish Capitol of the World," each year sponsors the International Horseradish Festival on the first weekend in June in a local park. Activities include horseradish golf, a fun walk-and-run, a horseradish eating contest, and many other activities as well as equipment exhibits and processor displays of bottled sauces.

Horseradish Sauce

If you grow horseradish, clean, trim, and store the whole roots, tightly wrapped in plastic, in the refrigerator. Try to make only as much grated sauce as you need for a meal, serve in a glass dish, and return the rest to the coldest part of the refrigerator immediately. Store in a glass container with a plastic lid and use as soon as possible. Serve with a non-metal spoon. To horseradish lovers, the following recipe is the easiest way to enjoy this piquant root, but beware: It is *not* creamy or mellow. This is one that Charles Voigt contributed to *Horseradish, Herb of the Year 2011* and Pat Crocker adapted, reprinted with permission here. Use a mature, two-year-old root (harvested after the first frost, if possible).

Cold water

½ cup crushed ice

1 fresh mature horseradish root, coarsely chopped (about 3 cups)

3 tablespoons vinegar or freshly squeezed lemon juice

2 tablespoons granulated sugar, optional

1 teaspoon salt

1. Add the cold water to the bowl of a large blender until the blades are covered. Add the ice, horseradish, vinegar, sugar if you're using it, and salt. Add more cold water until the level is about one-half of the volume of the blender.

2. Cover with the blender lid and process, from low to high, for about 30 seconds. Check the consistency and add more water if necessary; if it's too thick, then add a bit more water for better consistency. Process until the mixture is as fine as you desire. Spoon into a glass jar, add the lid, label and refrigerate. Freshly prepared horseradish will keep for several months but its pungency and flavor will decline over time.

Note: Processing horseradish indoors can get overpowering. It should be done outdoors or in an extremely well-ventilated area.

Jamaican Mint

Satureja viminea

Lamiaceae

S. viminea is a plant known by several names as it is in a type of name limbo at present. It is also known as Costa Rican mint bush, Jamaican peppermint, and serpentine savory. There are several other botanical names that refer to this plant, too, but I have chosen to go with *S. viminea*. In correspondence with Dr. Arthur Tucker he states, "*Satureja, Clinopodium*, and *Micromerica* need serious overhaul, probably with DNA, along with its relation to *Mentha*." Jamaican mint is native to Costa Rica, Jamaica, Cuba, and Hispaniola, an island in the Lesser Antilles. It grows in densely wooded areas in shale, in ravines, and gravelly streambeds. In its native area it will grow to ten feet tall. It is used in infusions, especially for the treatment of insomnia. No matter what the name is, Jamaican mint is a worthwhile plant to grow. Its beauty doesn't lie in its name but in what it is.

Description—Culture—Growing

Jamaican mint is a beautiful aromatic shrub with small white flowers. It prefers a moist and rich, but well-drained, soil and will grow well in full sun or partial shade. In the garden, it will grow to about three feet in height or large if given the proper growing conditions. Its glossy green leaves are darker when they're mature. Their aroma is similar to that of pennyroyal. Being a tropical plant (a tender perennial here), it needs to be protected when it gets below 45 degrees F, and it should be brought indoors in cold regions for the winter months. In the winter months the Jamaican mint is kept in my basement directly in front of the south-facing window where it receives ample light. I let it dry between waterings and when dry water thoroughly until a small amount appears in the saucer. The plant I have growing on my deck is very bushy and vigorous. It grew from a small plant in a three-inch pot in May to eighteen inches by twelve inches by late August. I have not seen it bloom; so far, it's just lots of lush foliage.

Propagation

In late winter plants will push out new growth and this is the optimum time to take cuttings. With sharp pruners snip two- and one-inch cuttings from the tips of new growth and stick them into a mixture of equal amounts of peat moss and perlite. They will root in ten to fourteen days when bottom heat is provided at a temperature of approximately 80 degrees F. I have seen reference for sowing seeds but since mine do not flower I have not used this method. Cuttings are really easy to root.

Uses

Jamaican mint is used seldomly, and I do not see much reference to it in cooking. Occasionally it is referenced to use the leaves, fresh or dried, added to water when cooking string beans, in soups and stuffing, added to sauces for veal or poultry, and in egg dishes and salads. The leaves are steeped in water and drunk as a tea in Jamaica.

Jasmine, Star

Trachelospermum jasminoides

Apocynaceae

Often known as Chinese star jessamine, star jasmine is native to eastern and southeastern Asia, Japan, Korea, southern China, and Vietnam. I had been growing this plant thinking it was a true jasmine until recently. Then, when I began to research it, I discovered it is in the genus *Trachelospermum*; for the past several years it has had the wrong name linked to it. Its best attribute is its extremely fragrant, showstopping flowers.

Description—Culture—Growing

Star jasmine makes an excellent container plant for a sunny location on the deck or patio. Some say the aroma is nutmeg-scented. It is not a true jasmine, but the scent of the flowers is very similar. It is a woody climber with opposite leaves, evergreen, and very fragrant. I've been growing it in a container measuring twelve inches by twelve inches, and each spring I remove it from its pot, shave off about three inches of the roots, and remove soil from its sides and bottom. Then it is transplanted back in the same container as I add new soil to replace the old that was removed. When a stem is cut a milky sap leaks out so place a newspaper under it to keep the sap off the floor. The egg-shaped foliage is dark green and shiny, pointed on both ends, and the creamy white flowers are

curved backward. Its flowers are arranged in clusters, and they are waxy, starlike, five petaled, and measure one inch in diameter. Flowers occur in early June and continue through July. I love to sit next to this plant and enjoy the sweet fragrance it emits during the days and evenings. In a container star jasmine grows to three feet by three feet; just keep it trimmed. At times the plant is susceptible to scale. As soon as the sticky sap is seen on the plant spray it with insecticidal soap every three days for about two weeks to rid it of scale.

When cold temperatures move in, usually in early October, I move the star jasmine to the south window in my basement where it thrives all winter. I usually clip it once during the winter to keep it from rambling. Keep it moist during the growing season to ensure it doesn't get too dry but allow the surface to dry out between waterings.

Plant star jasmine in a container large enough to insert a small trellis for the vines to grow upon. As it grows tie the vines to the trellis so it doesn't grow sporadically out of bounds. In spring when it is brought outdoors, shield it from direct sun for a few days and gradually acclimate it to full sun—this is needed to prevent the leaves from scorching. Other cultivars can be found with variegated, bronze, and narrow-leaved forms.

Propagation

Propagate this plant by softwood cuttings in the spring. Bottom heat of 70 to 75 degrees F is ideal to root the cuttings.

Uses

I love to enjoy the fragrance and beauty of this plant each summer on my deck! Star jasmine is a useful plant with perfume that is extracted from the flowers. Another benefit is unusual in that bast fiber is made from star jasmine as well as many other plants such as hemp, flax, linden, and milkweed. The strong fiber bundles are from the outer portion of the bark or stems. There is a process for obtaining the fiber and this is known as retting. Textiles, carpet, burlap, paper sacks, and rope are just several of the products you will find incorporating bast fiber.

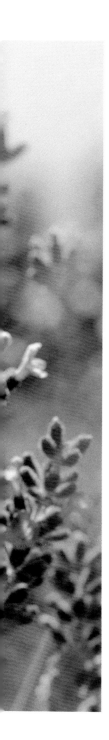

Lavender

Lavandula

Lamiaceae

The etymology of the genus *Lavandula* and its common name "lavender" was once believed to be derived from Latin word *lavare*, meaning "to wash." It is more likely that *Lavandula* is derived from the Latin word *livere*, meaning "to be livid or bluish." *L. stoechas* was used by the Romans and Greeks medicinally, but not in baths. In early times there were many mentions of lavender; it is an herb that has been highly valued through the ages. Lavender plants were grown in cottage gardens, which were valued for all aspects of domestic economy. The Abbess Hildegard of Bingen (1098–1179) had many talents including being a musician and a theologian, as well as an herbalist. She is given credit for writing about *Lavandula* in *Physica*, which was a handbook for healing. It was written in German and established the path for botanical studies in the German language over the next four centuries. In it she discussed lavender's medicinal properties and recorded the results of her findings. In *Physica*, Abbess Hildegard refers to the "strong odor and the many virtues of the plant" in the "De Lavandula" and "De Spica" sections. She also mentions a lavender-flower wine as a liver remedy. Lavender was said to have been in Burgundy in 1300 and was planted in the royal garden in Paris.

Description—Culture—Growing

Lavender is sought after for its endless fragrance. In the retail trade, lavender plants are grown as ornamentals in the garden for their shape, fragrance, and flower color. There was many a time, when

Jim and I owned our herb farm, that a customer would ask for lavender to grow as they had recently seen them in France growing in fields. They wanted to do the same in Minnesota. My reply was that it would be a dream if we could do that in the Upper Midwest, but it was not possible. Sure, you can grow several of the *L. angustifolia* cultivars, but unfortunately, they will not last for years and will eventually succumb to our environment. My recommendation in recent years has been to grow the tender perennial varieties such as those listed here in containers and enjoy their flowers all season long. They are fairly successful if you choose to overwinter them in the house or home greenhouse or, if you don't, just make a trip to the local herb farm or nursery to purchase new plants in spring. The beauty of these tender lavenders is that, once they begin to flower, they'll do so continually until a hard frost. They are spectacular and so fragrant when their foliage is brushed. Plant three to five in a container and enjoy the fragrant flowers. Lavenders are not often bothered by insect pests, although they may occasionally attract the spittlebug, *Philaenus spumarius*, which is about one-quarter inch in size. They overwinter as eggs that have been laid on host plants in the fall, and in the spring, tiny orange nymphs emerge from the eggs. While feeding, the nymphs produce a foamy spittle or froth that protects them from predators and drying out. If they are a nuisance to you they can easily be washed off with the garden hose, but I've never seen them to be a bother or to damage plants.

Propagation

Several lavenders may be grown from seed but cultivars should be propagated from cuttings to ensure that they are identical to the parent. I take cuttings from new growth of the varieties listed here in late February. I root them in a greenhouse (it is slightly more difficult to do this in your home). A hormone powder is recommended as a dip for the cuttings. Place them in a soilless mix of one-third peat moss and two-thirds perlite. Drainage is very important when growing lavender since the cuttings will rot if they are kept too moist. I mist the cuttings for three or four days and then reduce that to two to three times per week. This, of course, depends on the amount of sunlight provided and, as always, bottom heat is recommended.

Uses

Lavender is widely used in some form to soothe aching muscles, for headaches, relief of sinus issues, easing aching muscles, for a massage, and at bedtime by placing a few drops on a pillow to help sleep. Lavender is most often used for fragrance, and I always make sure to purchase a good quality essential oil of this herb. Some grow lavender for potpourri, others, to use fresh in bouquets. In culinary use, organic lavender flowers are used in herbal teas, cookies, ice cream, to flavor wine and simple syrups, and even as a spice rub for beef and lamb. Lavender oil at 20 ppm is considered GRAS (Generally Recognized As Safe), by the U.S. Food and Drug Administration. Lavender essential oil is often used in hospitals and nursing homes, as well as dentist offices, for aromatherapy to calm patients. Lavender is added to the bath in salts and placed in diffusers to scent a room instantly. Soaps, facial oils, floral waters, and perfume are other uses for lavender. In the early 1970s I was shown a lavender wand by an early mentor of mine, Bernice Anderson. She asked me to her home to make lavender wands—they looked simple to make and they smelled so wonderful—so I thought, "I can do this." Bernice gathered the lavender flowerheads, tying them together at their base, turning the stems upside down (to enclose the flowers), and began weaving a ribbon in and out. She made it look so easy and I proceeded to make one. But it wasn't as simple as it looked, and mine just never did turn out. Some people are wandmakers and some aren't. My friend Patty Kenny is one of those who is a pro at making lavender wands. Patty's instructions are listed here, and they are so complete and concise I am planning to try again.

Patty Kenny's Lavender Wands

"Many people suggest only making wands with lavender that is in bud. Depending on the weather, that does not give you many wandmaking days in June and July. My goal for a favorite herb shop was to make one hundred wands in a season, and I tried to make at least ten a week throughout the summer. When cutting lavender stems, take a tall vessel and fill with one to two inches of warm water. Remove the leaves from the stems, one stem at a time, saving the leaves to use in potpourri. I prefer sitting in the shade on a bench next to the garden. Keep the vase on the porch or in the house in a cool place. This way you can keep them for several days while making the wands. Over time, as the bottoms of the stems degrade, the water should be changed and the stems re-cut. After being cut, the blossoms continue to open naturally (and cooler temperatures will slow this process). The blossoms tend to fall off faster in places without natural light. It is always a good idea to experiment and find your own way."

How to Make a Lavender Wand

15 to 30 long (8- to 12-inch) stems of fresh lavender for each wand

½- or ¼-inch-wide ribbon

1. **To begin:** Choose an odd number of flower stalks. No matter how many it is, the number of stalks you choose to weave has to be an odd number. Therefore, if you have nineteen stalks, go over and under each. If you want to go over two at a time, letting go of one, leaving eighteen, you'll have an odd number of nine. You can increase the number of stalks to make a fatter wand; i.e., weaving over two stalks at a time you would be able to include a total of thirty stalks or fifteen "go-arounds."

2. **Preparing the stems:** Cut the stem bottoms so the length of each stem is the same. Align the bunch of lavender blossoms together with their "necks" somewhat touching. Use your fingers to roll and pinch the bunched necks to reduce the amount of cellular fluid, leaving the fibrous, cellulose strands. I learned from a fellow teacher to use needle-nose pliers to make this stage of lavender wandmaking easier and reduce time and pain. Gently, but firmly, press the bunch of necks, all at a time, between the pliers, turning them around and around as a group, to make sure all are massaged. The neck is the place under the most lavender blossom whorls. If necessary, remove a lower whorl of blossoms remembering that it naturally creates a weak place in the stem. The weaving can strengthen that place.

3. **The ribbon or weaver:** Select the ribbon color you like. Don't cut the ribbon; use a loose pocket, for a ribbon spool, and let it inch out, little by little. A short end will be hidden as much as possible in the center of the bunch that will eventually come out after you are finished weaving; it will be used to make a bow. Measure the tail by estimating the length of the final wand and tie the ribbon tightly under the neck accordingly; give yourself a couple of extra inches. Hide the shorter tail of the ribbon inside the bunch of stalks before the "fold over" (see photo #3). The rest of the ribbon that's wrapped around ribbon spool is the "weaver."

4. **The fold over:** With the weaver in your right hand, turn over and hold the blossom group in the palm of your left hand, up high, and give it a twirl. See which stems want to naturally fall down over the blossom group. Look over the entire wand and see where it can be evened out. Bring out your ribbon weaver in a good starting place closest to the tie around the stalks. Re-cut the stalks at the bottom, without cutting the ribbon, to an even length again, being certain there is enough to cover the blossom group after the fold over. It helps them get less in the way during the weaving.

5. **The process:** Weaving the first two rows determines whether you have counted your stalks and woven correctly. Compensate if needed, but it feels better if the over-and-under goes in sequence. Begin with over and under, travel down and around enjoying the challenge of lavender tightening the ribbon around the stems and making sure the blossoms stay underneath the ribbon. You'll tighten things up with a pointy wooden skewer later; you will get used to how much tension is needed along the way. The learning is in the doing, as is often the case in most things. When the group of blossoms is covered, start thinking about how you want to start finishing the wand handle. My favorite way is to tighten as the weaving gets under the blossom bulge, so find and bring out the shorter ribbon tail, leave it under the blossom group, and spiral the weaver down around the handle bottom and back up to the ribbon tail. Tightly tie them together (ask someone to hold the woven wand head or hold it between your knees) and make a bow.

6. **Additional ribbon information:** Since ribbon widths and colors may be changed midstream, here are further instructions on this process. After 3-5-7, or your choice, of go around spiral weavings, lock the weaver to the left with the fingers of your left hand and bring in the end of the new ribbon. Insert it in the space between the lavender stems toward the center, carefully but firmly, with a bamboo skewer or the flat blade of a pair of scissors. Next, circle the first weaver over top and back to the locking position and down to hide among the blossoms under the stems. The new ribbon becomes your second weaver for as long as you want; you can alternate the new second ribbon with the first, cut it to make what I call a "flag," or hide the cut end tightly inside the blossom bulge. The wand is finished with the first ribbon, the one with which you started out.

7. **Finishing:** Allow the wand to dry; a paper bag, with the wand inside, placed in the back of an automobile works great. It takes a full week or two for a wand of thirty-four stems to dry. Things shrink and bows relax, and I've learned to tack them with a couple stitches with thread of similar ribbon color. You also put a couple stitches through the crossed ribbon at the bottom of the wand handle. Voilà!

Lavenders to Grow

FERNLEAF LAVENDER

L. multifida

L. multifida is native to the European mainland and distributed from the western Mediterranean area, including southern Spain and Portugal, to the southern Mediterranean parts of Morocco, Algeria, Tunisia, and Libya. The plant is recognized by its unique stems of divided leaves; it flowers continuously with dark lavender blossoms. It is cultivated as an ornamental and is propagated from seed and softwood cuttings. Rex Talbert advises that one key in identifying this lavender is to look very closely at the shape of the leaf; it is quite distinctive from other lavenders. Planting lavender in containers allows cold climate gardeners to bring it indoors and enjoy the flowers further into the fall. The flower stems tower far above the foliage, and it is amazing to watch butterflies land on the flowers when there is a breeze. It is as though they are dancing.

FRINGED LAVENDER

L. dentata

This species has been described as being from Yemen, the eastern part of its distribution. It is an evergreen perennial (tender in the frost areas) and will flower almost continuously throughout the growing season if it's kept clipped. The violet-blue flowers are produced

on multiple, unbranched spikes. There are two
varieties of fringed lavender: one has leaves that
are gray (native to Arabia and the Middle East),
and the other has leaves that are bright green
(native to Iberia). It is easily propagated from
cuttings. Both the leaves and flowers of fringed
lavender are fragrant; in fact, it is easy to identify
by its finely toothed (dentate) leaves that have a
rich, aromatic scent. Its aroma is different from
most other lavenders and, according to Brownlow
(1963), has a "warm scent of a balsamic blend
of lavender and rosemary." When dried, the
oils remain in the foliage and create a pleasing
fragrance when added to potpourri.

'GOODWIN CREEK GREY' LAVENDER

L. x *ginginsii* 'Goodwin Creek Grey'

'Goodwin Creek Grey' lavender, a cross between
L. dentata and *L. lanata*, is a striking, small woody
shrub that should be more known to gardeners. It
grows very well in containers. The deeply toothed
(although some are entire), fragrant foliage feels
like velvet. The flower color is a rich violet-purple
that contrasts with silvery gray leaves, which are
very similar to *L. dentata*, but which are a lot larger
and whiter in color when they're mature. It blooms
continuously starting in early spring and has
been known to keep pushing out fragrant flowers
through the winter months in very mild areas.
Mature plants reach thirty-six inches in height,
producing conical flowers on slender

six- to eight-inch stems. It was introduced by Jim Becker of Goodwin Creek Gardens, Williams, Oregon, in 1991. *L. x ginginsii* is named in honor of Baron Frédéric Charles Jean Gingins de la Sarraz (1790–1863).

Jim Becker's 'Goodwin Creek Grey' Lavender

"In the late 1980s it began with a twenty-year-old *Lavandula dentata* topiary I had been growing. Dotti (my wife) and I discovered a small seedling, one-half inch or less, growing under this topiary. I was going to discard it, but Dotti thought it was unusual and different, and we kept it. It was getting large, and after two or three years we decided that it was an unusual lavender. We assumed it was a hybrid crossed between *L. dentata* and *L. lanata*. In 1991, a new botanical name was assigned with 'Goodwin Creek Grey' as the cultivar of this hybrid. We named it 'Goodwin Creek Grey' after the stream that ran through our property.

"If you see a plant named this, it should be the same plant from our stock (mother) plants. We never collected seed nor tried to grow it from seed. It is propagated from pliable, semi-soft cuttings rooted in straight perlite without hormones. Cuttings need heat, about 65 degrees F, no matter what time of year it is. In approximately four to six weeks roots form. It wasn't our intent to breed anything—it was just a chance seedling we found, and we've never seen anything quite like it. It grows well in Southern California and Arizona. It blooms eleven months of the year. In the southeastern part of the country it thrives where other lavenders have difficulty because of the heat and humidity. It is hardy to approximately 25 degrees F.

"There is a greenhouse grower that is promoting it as an indoor lavender to grow for a small greenhouse or warm sunroom. They say it blooms in the winter."

Lemongrass

Cymbopogon citratus

Poaceae

Lemongrass is from an area comprising Malaysia, Indonesia, New Guinea, the Philippines, and Brunei. It is mainly grown and used in Bali, Cambodia, Indonesia, Laos, Malaysia, Singapore, Sri Lanka, Thailand, and Vietnam. It would be a dream to see it growing wild in these areas.

Description—Culture—Growing

Grow lemongrass as a tender perennial in northern climates. In other areas much farther south in the United States it is a perennial. In the northern climates it is grown in gardens or in containers, attaining a height of two to three feet. It tolerates light shade but prefers full sun. Lemongrass is known as *xa* in Vietnamese and *takrai* in Thai. It is a common herb used to infuse sauces, soups, and curries, and to marinate meats and fish. The pale green, narrow, long leaves are characterized by the presence of silica thorns aligned on the leaf edges, which give a scratchy, rough feeling to one's fingers. In India, *C. citratus* is used both as a medicinal herb and in perfumes. Records of the medicinal use of lemongrass oil in India date back more than 2,000 years, though its distillation started only in 1890. Early in the 1950s India was a major producer of lemongrass oil in world trade, but this has now changed, as Guatemala, China, Mexico, and Bangladesh have developed large-scale lemongrass cultivation.

Propagation

Lemongrass is propagated by clump division. At the end of a growing season, if it's been grown in a container, bright yellow roots will fill the entire container and the plant will be full of foliage. This is a good time to divide the clump, but you will need a small saw to cut the clump apart. When it comes to this I prefer an electric Sawzall. In the greenhouse we used to cut clumps apart with a small handsaw, and it took *far* too long. We grew weary from all the sawing. One year an employee, Gary, said he knew how to make this task easier; sure enough, he came in with a Sawzall, which took no time at all and worked perfectly. After dividing the clump into pieces transplant them into a potting mix that is one-third potting mix, one-third peat moss, and one-third perlite; the divisions prefer a very light mix in order to root and continue growing.

Uses

Lemongrass is an essential ingredient in Asian cooking and is a well-known ingredient in lemongrass soup. The fleshy inner part of the stem is finely sliced or pounded to a paste and eaten raw. Its flavor is released by bruising the stem. Its lemony and gingery aromas complement the flavor of nearly all dishes. Young stems are cut at their base and added while cooking. The tough outside layers are peeled to get to the tender part of the plant. Choose those with fat bulbs; there will be more of it to use. The stalks will remain fresh for two to three weeks if they're stored in a plastic bag in the vegetable compartment of a refrigerator. Or, better yet, mince the lemongrass immediately, place that in a sealable plastic bag, and freeze. Frozen lemongrass will keep four to five months. Finely minced lemongrass is added to marinades, curries, and salads. Bigger pieces of the lower stem are generally used in broths and soups. In Australia, lemongrass is cultivated in order to add aroma to dishwashing liquids and the extracted oil, which contains the citral that gives it the lemon aroma, is used in soaps, cosmetics, and flavorings.

Mai Pham's Lemongrass
akrai in Thai, *xa* in Vietnamese

"How do I even begin to describe my love for lemongrass? It's my go-to herb when I want to cook up something really special, or when I want to give pizzazz to leftovers. With its long stalks, wrapped and bound together like an onion, and its long, elongated leaves that easily may be mistaken for an ordinary grasslike plant, lemongrass is indeed a unique and distinctive herb. Used throughout Asia and especially in Southeast Asian cuisine, it's often used to make curry pastes and marinades as well as stir fries and salads, such as Thai Green Curry, Lemongrass Chicken, and Thai Beef Salad.

"The most common way of handling this fibrous herb is to finely chop it. Using a sharp knife, cut a stalk into thin slices first, and then finely mince it. When it's added to spice pastes such as curry paste, lemongrass imparts bold flavors especially when you bite into a small piece. Another technique is to cut a stalk into four-inch lengths and smack them with a knife before adding to food. Or allow the stalks to simmer with and perfume a soup or stew; remove the stalk after cooking. Or try sucking on the stalks as they're irresistibly flavorful and sweet. In raw form, either minced or thinly sliced, lemongrass is lovely in salads, brightening all flavors with its refreshing citrusy and gingery undertones.

"If you're an herb lover like me, the next time you get your hands on healthy-looking stalks, try rooting them in water. If you're lucky, within several weeks of regularly changing the water and adding some root booster, the plant should develop roots. Transfer the rooted stalk to a pot or plant in the ground with ample sun (mulch in the winter). With a little love, the magic of lemongrass will slowly but surely grace your table."

Lemongrass Lemonade

This recipe makes a good, strong lemonade sweetened by a lemongrass-infused syrup. It's a delicious nonalcoholic drink, especially when the weather warms.

1 cup granulated sugar

2 stalks lemongrass, cut into ½-inch pieces and bruised lightly with the back of a knife

3 cups water

Garnish
1 lemon, thinly sliced

juice of 3 lemons

juice of 2 limes

pinch of salt

2 cups ice

2 stalks lemongrass, cut into 2-inch pieces

1. Combine the sugar, lemongrass, and water in a medium saucepan and bring to a boil over high heat. Stir to dissolve the sugar. Reduce the heat to low, and simmer 20 minutes. Remove from the heat and let sit for 1 hour.

2. Strain the cooled syrup into a glass pitcher. Add the lemon juice, lime juice, and salt to the syrup. Stir well and add the ice.

3. Serve the lemonade in tall glasses. Garnish with the lemon slices and lemongrass pieces.

Lemon Verbena

Aloysia citriodora

Verbenaceae

Native to Chile, Argentina, and Peru, lemon verbena grows as a fragrant shrub ten to fifteen feet tall. That is something I cannot imagine since in my Midwestern garden I am happy when it grows three to four feet tall. It is also known as cidron, herb Louisa, real vervain, sweet verbena, and verveine citronella. Lemon verbena leaves have a heavy aroma, similar to that of a lemon, due to its content of essential oils. Some say the Spanish conquistadors took it to Spain in the 1700s and it became naturalized in Europe. Around this same time, it was introduced to North America by a New England sea captain who brought it from Chile. In 1864, the Emperor Maximilian (1832–1867), emperor of Mexico from 1864–1867, and his wife, the Empress Carlotta, planted lemon verbena in the royal gardens of Montezuma's palace in Mexico, naming it "Yerba Louisa" after Carlotta's mother, the queen of Belgium. In past times, it was a common practice to include a sprig or two in flower bouquets and in finger bowls. Lemon verbena is used commercially in herbal tea mixtures, although it is of minor economic importance.

Description—Culture—Growing

This prize plant is hands down a favorite herb of mine. I love it! My husband, Jim, says it's his favorite, too, but whose it was first is debatable. It will uplift you with its fragrance, warm you with its leaves in teas, and tantalize your taste buds when it's added to grilled chicken. If you or a friend are perhaps not in the best of moods, all you need to do is cut a sprig of lemon verbena, relax, and inhale! Say no more. It is a woody plant with short-stalked leaves mostly arranged in whorls of three or sometimes four, two to four inches in length by one inch wide. The leaves are pointed lanceolate and light green. The flowers are not very showy, and the small lavender blooms are borne on slender terminal spikes three to five inches long. Full sun and well-drained soil are

what it prefers. In northern climates it is grown in the garden or containers. It doesn't winter well indoors as it is susceptible to a number of pests; it's easier just to purchase a new plant the following spring.

Propagation

Cuttings root readily but care needs to be taken in the first several days of cutting and sticking into the rooting medium. Cuttings should be three inches in length with the bottom leaves removed. Stick these into a moistened peat/perlite mixture after using a light hormone on the bottom ends of the cuttings. Lemon verbena leaves dry quickly. Keep in mind they need to be kept moist after transplanting and covered for several days until acclimated. I've not seen seed offered for lemon verbena.

Uses

The uses for lemon verbena are almost endless. Fruit cups, puddings, cakes, cookies, teas, and jellies are just the beginning. If you don't have fresh leaves of lemon verbena then dried ones harvested the previous fall work well. To harvest, cut large stems that are covered with leaves, wash them in a large bucket of cold water (don't use warm or hot water as you'll lose the oils and have a dirty tea), and lay them on a table outdoors to air-dry. Wrap the stem ends several times with a rubber band and hang them on a hook or kitchen cupboard door handle to dry. Usually it only takes three to four days because the leaves are paper thin. After they're dry, strip the leaves from the stems and store in glass jars for tea or potpourri. When you are ready to use the leaves, process them in a small food processor and then pour through a strainer. The leaves have a stringy type of vein down the center (the midrib), and it needs to be removed; straining takes care of this. Fresh or dried leaves are flavorful for teas and if they're added to vegetables whole, they can easily be removed after cooking. In addition to fruit and desserts, lemon verbena goes well with custards, fish, and poultry, as well as added to cookies, breads, salad dressings, and mushrooms. The essential oil is used in aromatherapy, perfumery, soaps, and cosmetics. The dried leaves of lemon verbena can also be added to a potpourri for scent.

Lemon Verbena Pound Cake

This is a lovely pound cake with a beautiful, fine-grained texture. It is unbeatable with fresh sliced strawberries or fresh whole raspberries on the side. A dollop of whipped cream wouldn't be amiss either.

1 cup cake flour, plus more to flour the pan

½ teaspoon baking powder

¼ teaspoon sea salt

3 tablespoons finely chopped lemon verbena leaves (midrib removed from each leaf)

1 tablespoon grated lemon zest

Glaze
½ cup confectioners' sugar

½ cup unsalted butter, softened

1 cup granulated sugar

3 large eggs

1 teaspoon vanilla

2 tablespoons milk

2 tablespoons fresh lemon juice

Fresh lemon verbena leaves, optional

1 tablespoon fresh lemon juice

1. Preheat the oven to 325 degrees F.

2. Butter and flour a 3x5x3-inch loaf pan. Tap out any excess flour.

3. In a medium bowl, combine the 1 cup flour, baking powder, salt, lemon verbena, and lemon zest.

4. In a large mixing bowl, beat the butter and sugar until it's light and fluffy. Beat in the eggs, one at a time, beating well after each addition. Beat in the vanilla.

5. Add half the flour mixture and beat well to combine. Add the milk and lemon juice and beat. Add the remaining flour mixture and mix until just combined. Pour the batter into the prepared loaf pan. Spread the batter into the corners and smooth the top using a spatula. Bake in the preheated oven for 45 to 50 minutes or until a tester comes out clean. Cool the cake in the pan for 15 minutes, and then turn out onto serving plate to cool completely.

6. When you're ready to add the glaze, combine the confectioners' sugar and lemon juice in a small bowl; mix well. Drizzle over the cake. Decorate the edges of the cake with fresh lemon verbena leaves, if desired.

Beyond Rosemary, Basil, and Thyme

Theresa's Bouquet Garni Vinegar

2 quarts champagne or white wine vinegar

4 to 6 sprigs lemon verbena, cleaned and air-dried

4 stems Italian parsley, cleaned and air-dried

2 cloves garlic, peeled

2 jalapeño (or similar variety) peppers, deveined and seeded, cut in half

4 stems dill, cleaned and air-dried

4 stems rosemary, cleaned and air-dried

Lemon zest or 4 thin lemon slices

8 to 10 stems French or 'Silver Posie' thyme, cleaned and air-dried

1. Divide all the dry ingredients equally into two 1-quart glass jars (the jars will be packed). Add vinegar to each jar until it reaches the bottom of the top rim. Cap with a lid (preferably plastic).

2. The vinegar is ready to use in 1 week but it can sit for 2 to 3 weeks. Strain the ingredients from the jars and fill decorative containers for personal use and for gifts. Use this bouquet garni vinegar for sautéing vegetables, over cold, cooked vegetables, in salad dressings, and wherever you want extra flavor!

Susan Betz's The Pleasures of Potpourri

"The natural fragrance and beauty of a potpourri crafted from flowers and herbs harvested from your summer garden will lift your spirits throughout the cold winter months.

"There are two traditional ways of making potpourri, the dry method or the moist. The moist method is the oldest way. Partially dried herbs and flowers are packed and preserved in alternate layers of salt in covered ceramic pots and then set aside to cure or rot for weeks or months; this method yields a potpourri that is more fragrant but lacks visual appeal. It's no surprise the original French word means 'rotten pot.' The dry method described here is more popular with potpourri crafters today. The dried herbs and spices may include flower petals or blossoms, leaves, seeds, barks, and roots. Dried citrus peel is often added for color, texture, and aroma.

"Traditionally, flowers dominate potpourri mixtures, especially rose petals and lavender as they retain their fragrances the longest. Other colorful garden flowers to dry are bachelor buttons, Dianthus, marigolds, zinnias, hibiscus, peonies, and delphinium. Herbs chosen for scent may include rosemary, thyme, scented geraniums, sage, sweet marjoram, mint, artemisia, and lemon verbena.

"There are no precise rules in the choice or proportion of ingredients; creating a potpourri recipe is an art based on personal taste and discretion. You can use a recipe or follow your nose. Mixtures can depend solely on the natural scents of their ingredients, or they can be enhanced with fixatives and essential oils. Fixatives help capture and preserve volatile oils in the herbs and flowers and prolong the life of the potpourri. Essential oils are concentrated aromatic plant distillates.

"I like to follow my nose. My favorite mix is a refreshing citrus-scented potpourri based on a combination of dried lemon verbena, lemon geraniums, and lemon eucalyptus. I accent this mixture with marigold petals, orange peel, cloves, and orris root mixed with sweet orange oil. I grow these plants every year. As summer and fall progress, harvest the potpourri's herb ingredients, strip the foliage from the stems, and layer the leaves on screens to dry. I also dry orange, lemon, and lime peels. Store these in glass jars until ready to use."

Lovely Lemon Potpourri

6 tablespoons dried, cut, ground, and
sifted orris root

4 tablespoons whole cloves

2½ teaspoons sweet orange pure
essential oil (or another citrus
essential oil)

4 cups dried lemon verbena leaves

2 cups dried lemon eucalyptus leaves

2 cups dried scented geranium leaves

1 cup orange peel pieces

1 cup marigold petals

1. Blend the orris root, cloves, and essential oil in a quart glass jar. Set aside to "rest" for 3 to 4 days.

2. Combine the lemon verbena, eucalyptus, scented geranium, orange peel, and marigold petals in a large stainless steel mixing bowl. Mix thoroughly, and divide equally into two large glass jars. Divide the orris root mixture equally into these two jars.

3. Store the potpourri in the glass jars with tight-fitting lids for 4 to 6 weeks. Shake once or twice a week.

4. After 4 to 6 weeks, place this colorful and fragrant blend into sachet bags or display it in a bowl on the table.

Lovely Lemon Potpourri

Ingredients for the potpourri

Lovage

Levisticum officinale

Apiaceae

Lovage is native to the Mediterranean region, growing wild in the mountainous areas of the South of France, in northern Greece, and in the Balkans. The roots and fruit are aromatic, and act as a stimulant. Nicholas Culpeper wrote in *The English Physician* (1835), "It is an herb of the Sun, under the sign Taurus. If Saturn offend the throat (as he always doth if he be occasioner of the malady, and in Taurus is the Genesis) this is your cure....It is a known and much praised remedy to drink the decoction of the herb for any sort of ague, and to help the pains and torments of the body and bowels coming of cold. The seed is effectual to all the purposes aforesaid (except the last) and worketh more powerfully." Ancient Greeks often chewed the seeds to aid digestion. The perennial lovage is a forgotten herb that is useful in the kitchen in so many ways.

Description—Culture—Growing

Lovage is a robust plant that doesn't require much attention and is like an old friend appearing every spring when it emerges from the ground in April. I have enjoyed this beautiful plant in my garden for many years, and it surely tolerates our subzero Minnesota winters. Too few people are aware of its uses, and I enjoy bringing it to the forefront of herbs. Lovage is a towering plant, up to six feet, that is well placed in the back of the garden or along a fence so it will not overtake smaller plants. The leaves

are alternate and in threes, compound, deeply divided, and dark green with a flavor similar to celery. The greenish yellow flowerheads stand far above the main plant and eventually topple over from their weight. In mid-July cut lovage back to the ground with loppers or pruners. Don't worry—you aren't killing the plant, but merely forcing new growth that will begin in a few days, ready for a fresh new crop. The smaller stems can be used as straws for Bloody Marys, giving a hint of celery flavor as you sip the drink. The seeds attract birds, especially goldfinches. I can't imagine not having fresh lovage in the summer—it is a delight to smell and use.

Propagation

Plants in the garden will occasionally reseed though I have not found this to be a nuisance. Another method of increasing plants is to dig the clump in early spring as stalks are emerging, spray the roots clean with a garden hose, divide, and transplant back into the garden. Or give some transplants to other gardening friends.

Uses

The time to harvest lovage is in spring when it is about one and one-half foot tall. The foliage is fresh, and this is the ideal time to dry the leaves. One method I use is to cut the stems, wash them in cold water, and air-dry. Strip the leaves from the stems and place them in a single layer in a dehydrator, on a low temperature setting, watching it several times as the day goes on. After three or four hours the leaves likely will be dry. After the leaves are dry, place them in a food processor, whirl them, and then fill small glass bottles with the lovage. Store in a cabinet. After the plant is cut back and it grows again, you can do the same, always using new growth.

A friend recommended cooking with lovage and adding it to egg dishes; now I wouldn't be without it for any egg dish. Add chopped lovage leaves to soups and stock bases as well as to rice and vegetables. It is an interesting addition to stir-fried vegetables and even, summer squash. Chop lovage finely and add to buttered potatoes or to white sauces as well as to the Hollandaise sauce that drapes eggs Benedict. A favorite of mine is to add fresh lovage to old-fashioned potato salad. And that's not just one tablespoon but three or four, though you should consider that I don't just make a small bowl of potato salad but rather, I use five or more pounds of potatoes. In the growing season use fresh lovage and when the weather turns cold, it's so handy to have prepared the dried form to have on hand for cooking. Lovage seeds can be added whole to candy, cakes, pickles, and biscuits.

Swiss Chard Egg Bake

Fresh farm eggs, Swiss chard from the garden or farmers' market, and lovage make this a delectable dish for any meal. Choose from any of the colored chard varieties for this recipe.

8 ounces penne pasta

2 packed cups chopped (1-inch pieces) Swiss chard

4 eggs, beaten

1¼ cups cottage cheese

1 cup grated Parmesan cheese (plus some for serving)

2 tablespoons chopped fresh lovage

Sea salt and freshly cracked black pepper, to taste

Extra-virgin olive oil

1. Preheat the oven to 350 degrees F.

2. In a large pot of boiling water, cook the pasta to al dente, drain in a colander, reserving the water. When the pasta has drained, transfer it to a large bowl.

3. Cook the Swiss chard in the same water for a minute or so, drain, and add to the pasta. Combine the eggs, cottage cheese, Parmesan cheese, and lovage in a large bowl, and mix well. Add the pasta and chard, seasoning with the salt and pepper.

4. Place the chard mixture into an olive oil-greased 11x8-inch glass baking dish. Smooth the top with the back of a spoon, and cover with aluminum foil. Bake 35 to 40 minutes, or until a knife comes out clean when inserted in the center. Set aside to cool for 5 minutes before cutting and serving. Cut into squares and serve with more Parmesan cheese.

Mexican Oregano

Lippia graveolens

Verbenaceae

Mexican oregano is not a true oregano of the genus *Origanum* that typically comes from the Mediterranean coast. Rather, its home is Mesoamerica, a cultural area including the lower two-thirds of Mexico, all of Guatemala, Belize, and the western eighth of Honduras. As the invading Spaniards in the sixteenth century left their cultural homeland and lived in a different land they longed for food from their native land so they practiced fusion cooking and combined cuisines from different cultures. Garlic was replaced by *Bignonia aequinoctialis*, the garlic vine, and oregano flavors were substituted by *Lippia graveolens* and *Poliomintha bustamanta*. It goes on and on with other substitutions for bay, tarragon, and peppers. There is a large distinction between the European (*Origanum* spp.) and Mexican (*Lippia* sp.) oreganos. Mexican oregano is considered an economically important plant, with Mexico as one of the main exporters of oregano (mainly to the United States and the European Union) in the world, representing 35 to 40 percent of the international market. In Mexico it is used for flavoring and also for medicinal use. The essential oil will vary among plant populations in different environmental conditions, and *L. graveolens* harvested in high aridity regions has higher essential oil yield.

Description—Culture—Growing

It is a popular herb for flavoring foods in Mexico, and there it grows as a shrub up to six feet tall in its native habitat where it is adapted to rocky slopes and arid conditions. The oval-shaped leaves are small, and the shrublike plant grows in full sun. It is closely related to lemon verbena and has a flavor similar to oregano but much stronger and with a bite. There are other plants that share the common name of Mexican oregano, including *Poliomintha longiflora*, *Lippia berlandieri*, and *Plectranthus amboinicus*. Although not widely known in North America, this "oregano" is a wonderful plant for any herb gardener. It grows up to three feet tall in northern climates. Its branches are narrow and arching. The more it is clipped the more it grows and it dries very well—either hung in small branches by the stems or the leaves dried on cookie sheets. The half-inch leaves are dark green, the tiny white flowers have yellow centers. Container plants prefer full sun and a well-drained soil. On hot summer days I water the plants once daily, and I fertilize every two to three weeks. Usually I am successful in wintering Mexican oregano indoors in my basement with a south-facing window. It prefers the same growing conditions as bay or rosemary.

Propagation

Propagate Mexican oregano by taking cuttings from stock (mother) plants in late February or early March. I have not grown it by seed because tip cuttings work very well. If you do obtain seed it is a good idea to pretreat the seeds to stimulate germination. Do this by mixing the seeds in a moist peat/sand mixture and refrigerate for two to three months. However, I have not seen seeds offered of this oregano.

Uses

The intense oregano aroma is preferred by many over European oregano, and the flavor is sharper and more pungent than that of *Origanum*. It is added to fish, sausages, tomato sauce, and any other dish requiring a strong oregano flavor. In Mexico it is customary to dry and then toast the leaves to a dark brown color. The herb is sometimes called *té de pais* ("country tea") because the dried leaves are brewed into an herbal tea. It is also added to salsas, pozole (Mexican-style hominy soup, usually prepared with pork), and rajas (roasted and seasoned chile strips used as filling for tortillas or quesadillas or as a base for more complex dishes). It complements many dishes including pinto beans and soups. It enhances butter when it's served over fresh sweet corn, red and green peppers, and pinto beans, and in vinaigrettes. During the growing season I am cutting and drying the leaves as much as possible, and I combine this herb with 'Hilltop Herb Farm' oregano for a wonderful combination. Keep the leaf whole until ready to use—the oils dissipate quickly when crushed.

Creamy Roasted Tomato Soup

At summers end when you have a crop of tomatoes that you don't know how to use, here's a tasty recipe to make. Heirloom tomatoes are the most flavorful. 'Sungold' is a very tasty cherry tomato and works well in this recipe. Use more or fewer poblano peppers depending on your heat preferences.

8 large tomatoes

3 cloves garlic, peeled and mashed or finely chopped

1 tablespoon fresh Mexican oregano, chopped

6 to 8 medium-sized fresh poblano peppers

2 tablespoons extra-virgin olive oil

1 medium sweet onion, chopped

5 cups vegetable broth

6 ounces goat cheese

1 teaspoon sea salt

1 teaspoon freshly ground black pepper

1 cup half-and-half

Garnish

3 to 4 cherry tomatoes, quartered

½ cup cubed goat cheese

Marjoram or chopped fresh basil leaves

113

Mexican Oregano

1. Preheat the oven (or outdoor grill) to broil and position an oven rack on the highest level.

2. Roast the large tomatoes on a rimmed baking sheet under the broiler, turning once, until the skins burst and juice is coming out of the tomatoes. Cool, peel, and pour the juices with the tomatoes into a blender. Process to a smooth mixture. Set aside.

3. Roast the chiles in the oven under the broiler (or on the grill), turning frequently, for 10 to 15 minutes or until blackened on all sides. Place in a brown paper bag for 20 to 30 minutes. Peel off the skins and pull the stems and seedpods out. Rinse to remove bits of skin and seeds, discarding the skin and seeds, and chop into quarter-inch pieces. Set aside.

4. In a 5-quart Dutch oven heat the oil over medium heat. Add the onion and cook, stirring frequently, for 4 to 5 minutes or until lightly browned. Add the garlic and oregano, toss, and cook a minute or two longer. Add the poblanos and tomatoes and cook, stirring frequently, for 8 to 10 minutes or until thick and reduced.

5. Stir in the broth and simmer over low heat for 45 minutes. Season with the salt and pepper and add the half-and-half. Serve in bowls topped with cubes of goat cheese, marjoram or basil, and cherry tomatoes.

Mexican Tarragon

Tagetes lucida

Asteraceae

Tagetes is the botanical name for the multitude of marigolds that are ordinarily grown in the garden. Mexican tarragon is native to southern Mexico and Guatemala and is cultivated in El Salvador and Honduras. Spanish names for this plant are Yerbanis, anisillo, Santa Maria, and pericon. It is interesting that this plant is compared to French tarragon with similar flavor. There are plants that don't grow successfully in the northern climates and vice versa in the southern United States. French tarragon is difficult to grow in states such as Texas but there, Mexican marigold thrives. It was recommended to Madalene Hill as a tea by a Mexican woman. Hill recognized that the plant does indeed taste like French tarragon (*Artemisia dracunculus* 'Sativa'). Thanks to Madalene's persistence Mexican tarragon is now cultivated widely in Southwestern landscapes as a tarragon substitute.

Description—Culture—Growing

T. lucida grows eighteen to thirty inches tall and is an upright bushy plant. Clusters of single yellow flowers appear in midsummer and stay until the first frost. Leaves, deeply divided and toothed, are linear to oblong, about three inches long, shiny, and green. Later in summer it flowers with golden yellow heads at the ends of the stems. The flowers are easily pollinated by insects. In northern climates it is grown as an annual and is replanted each spring. By fall there is sufficient growth to harvest and dry for winter use.

Propagation

Mexican marigold is easily started indoors from seed in early spring and transplanted into the garden. In the South it reseeds, but not so in northern climates where it is a non-seeding annual. Sow seeds in a light peat/perlite mix and place in a warm location until they germinate, and then move them to a bright sunny window. I've also taken cuttings from new growth and even had them root in water in a glass container near a window.

Uses

It pairs well with corn, meats, and poultry. Chopped, it can be mixed with cheese or used in a spread. Leaves are added to salads, egg dishes, and poultry dishes, as well as vinaigrettes, herb butters, and vinegars. Some say it is a substitute for any dish where French tarragon is called for, but I am partial to French tarragon for my favorite recipes. Dried leaves keep well into the winter when French tarragon is not available. In Mexico the leaves and flowerheads are traditionally used in tea for a mild anise flavor.

Mint

Mentha spp.

Lamiaceae

In addition to mint traveling around in the garden, you may find that while doing so they may cross with one other and, invariably, it will get confusing. In reality there are not that many species of *Mentha*—about eighteen. They are native to many places around the globe: Europe, Asia, Australia, North America, North Africa, New Zealand, and Japan. In the horticulture industry the same mint will surely have several names by which it is known. Interesting also is the fact that chocolate mint is probably a peppermint. Some people think after whiffing the leaves it smells just like chocolate but, in fact, it is named so because the stems have a dark "chocolate" color. Traveling through Poland in the 1990s I recall seeing fields where mint was grown.

At the end of the field were large drying racks that were full of mint. After asking a local what it might be, he said it was peppermint. In the United States mint is susceptible to a number of diseases and insects and several plants are being bred for resistance. It is uncertain when a mint is named if it is a cross between species or where it came from unless there are accurate records. Botanists and horticulturists agree about mints and it is difficult to determine their identity.

Mints are great plants, and I don't know what I'd do without them. But finding a suitable home for them is important and can be a challenge. All mints are perennial and should not be planted directly into an herb bed because they are "friendly" and like to visit other parts of the garden. So it is a good idea to plant mints away from other plants or, better yet, pot them in a container to enjoy near the kitchen door. Just remember to plant *only* mint in the container—if planted with other herbs, mint will take over.

Description—Culture—Growing

When Shady Acres Herb Farm was in business, customers would ask for mint and I'd ask, "Which mint would you like?" The answer was mint—just mint! I went on to explain that there are many mints, and you need to decide on a particular flavor or scent. We would proceed to the mint bench, and then pinch and smell the many mints. Eventually, the customer decided upon a mint. For a home garden I wouldn't let nomenclature deter your enjoyment of mint; when your nose finds a good mint just grow it! Taxonomy aside, mint is a fascinating group of plants with so many fragrances, leaf textures, flowers, and uses.

Propagation

I recommend never growing any mints from seed because the end product will be variable. All mints that I've grown are maintained and propagated only by cuttings or root division. When mint is planted in the garden, it's a good idea to dig up part of the mint bed each spring, turn it over, and add new soil or compost. Mint roots tend to get thick and eventually part of the bed, usually the center, dies. By using the dig method, it renews the bed, and this should be done to all mints.

Uses

To preserve the flavor, dry mint stems in a humid-free area for about ten days or so. After they are dry, strip the leaves, place them in a glass bottle, and store until you're ready to use them. Keep leaves whole; that way more essential oils are preserved and are not lost if leaves are crushed too soon. When bunches of mint are hanging in the kitchen it is a delight—imagine fragrances of spearmint and orange mint—what a paradise! Mint makes a delightful tea and mojito, flavors tabbouleh and vinegar, and can be added to the bath water.

Mints to Grow

CORSICAN MINT

M. requienii

M. requienii is native to the islands of Sardinia (Italy), Montecristo (Italy), and Corsica (France). You would not recognize this as a mint; it looks like the houseplant called baby's tears until you bruise the leaves and smell the crème de menthe fragrance that comes from this tiny plant. Most mints are very aggressive and can quickly take over a garden. Not so with this little mint. Corsican mint is a miniature mat-forming plant with rounded, bright green leaves. The plant grows only one-quarter to one-half inch tall and spreads by threadlike stems that creep along the ground, rooting as it spreads. In southern climates it is particularly effective as an aromatic filler growing around stepping stones where light foot traffic releases its pleasing aroma. Minute lilac flowers bloom from the leaf axils in summer; just look closely as they are barely visible. It will tolerate full sun with sufficient moisture but it grows in partial shade. I like to plant it in small strawberry jars where, eventually, it will cover the entire planter. Or use it as a groundcover in fairy gardens. Richo Cech of Strictly Medicinal Seeds says, "Seed is very tiny and may be mixed with sand to afford even application. Strew on [the] surface of a pot and press in securely, keep evenly moist, in the light in a cool to warm temperature. Germination is in five to ten days. Grow the very fine seedlings on for some time, transplant as clumps into small pots, and when they have spread sufficiently to cover the surface of the pot, transplant out to the garden, pathway or rockery."

I was somewhat skeptical of the Corsican mint reseeding until recently. It died in early fall in the original container I had it planted it in. There wasn't one plant of this mint in any of the other pots. Spring came and I transplanted the herbs into containers after trimming the roots and adding new soil. After 6 weeks I noticed Corsican mint coming up in five of the containers in little clumps—all over. I'm convinced the seed germinated after the repotting, and that's where they came from. Seed was there from the dead plants.

It is very easy to divide the mat by cutting it with a sharp knife into small pieces and replanting; they will continue to grow.

'HIMALAYAN SILVER' MINT

M. longifolia 'Himalayan Silver'

'Himalayan Silver' mint is native from western Europe to India to South Africa. It is known by other names, including buddleia mint, horse mint, and silver mint. It is grown for its very long, beautiful spires of small, pale purple flowers and silvery grey leaves that are coarsely hairy with sparsely toothed edges. I prefer other mints to use for culinary purposes but the colorful leaves and flowers make up for its lack of flavor. It can reach up to three feet tall and is an excellent plant for butterflies and bees from late June into July. Since it is a desirable plant to grow for its beauty, it is worth finding a place for it in the garden. It is as easy to grow as any mint in partial shade and in full sun if the site is somewhat moister. To encourage new growth, mint should be cut back often. 'Himalayan Silver' mint is easy to multiply by root division in early spring as well as by cuttings.

Jim Mieseler's Spearmint

"From 1977 through 2016 we sold our herbs at the Minneapolis Farmers' Market and at our farm. It was 1991, and I had set up the sales display at the market and was visiting a local grower down the aisle from our stand. This grower had several pots of a mint, and I smelled a particular one. I immediately said, 'This is the old-fashioned mint I remembered as a child.' It far surpassed any spearmint we had been growing and ever since, it is the only spearmint we grew. Customers came and asked for it, saying it was the best mint and they couldn't find anything else like it anywhere. We didn't know what to call it but everyone referred to it as 'Jim's Mint' and that is the name we've had for it all these years."

JIM'S SPEARMINT

M. spicata 'Jim's Mint'

I grow a number of mints but my favorite for tea is spearmint, and for a mojito, it is *the* mint to use. It is important to find a good variety of spearmint to grow. Spearmint is refreshing and cooling, and spearmint is a useful herb. Its fresh leaves can be clipped and added to water for a nice summer drink. It is used to flavor green peas, new potatoes, and to make mint jelly. Dried spearmint leaves are used in herbal sleep pillows, sachets, and potpourri. It attains a height of twenty-four inches in the summer. Trim the flowers to maintain fresh green growth of stems and leaves.

Minted Cucumber Salad

Try 'Suyo Long' cucumbers in this tasty and easy-to-make recipe.

½ cup chopped walnuts

¼ cup chopped fresh spearmint

1 cup plain yogurt

2 cloves garlic, minced

1 tablespoon white wine vinegar

1 to 2 teaspoons honey

1 teaspoon sea salt

1 teaspoon ground coriander

2 large cucumbers, peeled, seeded, and
  diced

Combine the walnuts, spearmint, yogurt, garlic, vinegar, honey, salt, and coriander in a medium-sized bowl. Mix well and fold in the cucumbers.

ORANGE MINT

M. aquatica var. *citrata*

Orange mint is sweetly scented like citrus and its aroma lingers with you long afterward. It is a nice addition to fruit, especially pears, desserts, teas, and cold drinks. A favorite of mine is to add it to tussie mussies (miniature herbal nosegays) because of its delightful fragrance. The dark green leaves, with a hint of purple, are broad and round. In early spring the plant is somewhat reddish purple on new growth. Coincidentally, one day I was making deviled eggs and thought I'd try something new and added orange mint—voilà! A new flavor in the egg dishes and a crowd pleaser.

Moujean Tea

Nashia inaguensis

Verbenaceae

Nashia was originally thought to be native to the Island of Great Inagua, which is the third-largest island in the Bahamas. Inagua National Park covers a huge forty-five percent of the island. It is there that *Nashia* is known as moujean tea. It was found growing on the outskirts of Matthew Town nearly fifty years ago by Dr. John Popenoe, then-director of the Fairchild Gardens, Coral Gables, Florida. The plant is named after George Valentine Nash, a botanist who specialized in the flora of the Bahamas.

The following article came to me from correspondence with Dr. Brett Jestrow, director of collections, Fairchild Tropical Botanic Garden, in regard to where *Nashia* was previously thought to be native. It is excerpted from *Revision of the Caribbean Endemics Currently Placed in Nashia (Verbenaceae)* by Werner Greuter and Rosa Rankin Rodriguez, January 2016. "The distribution of *Nashia* proper is somewhat unusual. The species is known from three very local populations on Inagua (southernmost island in the Bahamas), Puerto Rico, and St. Croix in the Virgin Islands, thus skipping Hispaniola and Cuba. This slightly anomalous, disjunct area has, we believe, a plausible explanation. The

two *Nashia* populations of St. Croix and Puerto Rico grow in natural or semi-natural coastal thorn-scrub communities. On Great Inagua *Nashia* occurs on roadsides and in disturbed or inhabited sites, which is confirmed by collector's notes on various labels; and leaf morphology of the Bahamas plants is exactly the same as in those from the Virgin Islands. We therefore postulate that the Bahamas population was introduced to Matthew Town from St. Croix by man, presumably by some early settlers or their slaves, who used the plant for brewing their moujean tea." Dr. Jestrow concluded with, "Having personally seen *N. inaguensis* growing in Matthew Town, this makes a lot of sense as it is only found close to the settlement and is semi-cultivated."

Description—Culture—Growing

This aromatic small shrub has grey bark, spreading branches, and crinkled leaves that are small and bright green. Nestled in the foliage are minute white flowers. They are followed by glossy orange/yellow berries that turn black as the seed ripens. *N. inaguensis* has fruits of the same type as *Lantana* species. I have grown *Nashia* for ten years, and it is a unique plant that is not readily offered for sale.

It likes full sun and warm temperatures. It is essential to keep it indoors in the winter when temperatures dip below freezing. If the soil dries out too much it will drop its leaves, and you will think it is dead, but wait—water it and soon new leaves appear. That is a big hint to keep the plant moist during the winter months (which I sometimes forget). The plant on my deck is three feet tall and grows profusely each summer. The leaves have a pleasant, clean aroma that's somewhat lemony.

Propagation

When you see the woodiness of the plant you might think it would be impossible to root cuttings. In fact, in late winter, they root very easily with bottom heat in about two weeks.

Uses

According to Dr. Popenoe, "moujean" is a slang term for a person from Bermuda. Great Inagua has always been famous for its salt, as there is little rainfall and constant wind. The sun and wind evaporate the water, leaving the salt. Did the moujeans discover this plant and make tea from it? Dr. Popenoe could not conclude whether a tea was used for medicinal purposes or just for flavoring the slightly saline water that they probably had to drink on Inagua. He also noted that he added the green leaves and stem tips to boiling water. After a few minutes, the water turned green. When he tasted it, he said was like tasting 3-IN-ONE oil. He thinks he would prefer the taste of saline water, but perhaps this tea would be different if it were made with saline water! One won't know until one tries.

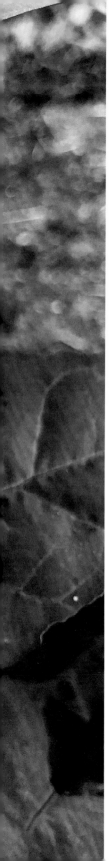

Orach

Atriplex hortensis

Amaranthaceae

The species A. *hortensis* is a native to Europe and Siberia. It is commonly naturalized on the Pacific Coast and less abundantly elsewhere in the United States. It has been traced to Tartary, the region of Eurasia that the Mongols took over in the thirteenth and fourteenth centuries. Orach is also known as butter leaves or mountain spinach and is a close relative of spinach.

Description—Culture—Growing

Orach is an annual that is cultivated as an edible green. Unlike most greens such as lettuce, orach will tolerate warm weather. Leaf colors vary from green, yellowish green, or red. Leaves are two to six inches long, opposite, and toothed. Its new growth resembles spinach, and when the leaves are cooked they do not lose color. Pinch off the flower buds to encourage branching and more young vegetative growth.

Propagation

Oftentimes seeds will drop, overwinter, and germinate the following spring. All varieties of orach are easily grown from seed, which germinate quickly. It can be sown indoors several weeks before transplanting outdoors, or you can sow it in the space where the plants will grow. They are easily cared for in good garden soil in a sunny location. Orach can be grown as a cut-and-come-again green by planting seeds in wide rows and thinning them to only a few inches apart.

Uses

Orach can be eaten raw as an addition in a salad or cooked quickly in water; add a little butter and seasoning. The younger leaves tend to be better for eating raw, while the more mature leaves make a good cooked spinach substitute. When cooking or meal planning, think of all the dishes in which you would normally use spinach, and substitute orach instead: pizza, stir fry, pasta, soup, risotto ... the list goes on. Just remember it has a slightly salty flavor, so you may need to cut back on the salt in your recipes. The leaves of red orach add a colorful pink to purple color to mixed salads.

Risotto with Orach

Risotto pairs well chicken or pork. Complete the meal by adding asparagus or roasted vegetables, and a side salad for a culinary delight.

1 tablespoon extra-virgin olive oil

¾ cup finely chopped red onion

2 cloves garlic, minced

1½ cups arborio rice

½ cup pinot noir

2 cups seafood or chicken stock

2 cups vegetable stock

¼ cup finely chopped orach

Sea salt and freshly ground black pepper

2 tablespoons minced fresh Italian parsley

½ cup Parmesan cheese

1. In a heavy 3-quart saucepan, heat the oil over medium-high heat. Add the onion and garlic, and sauté until they're translucent.

2. Stir in the rice and cook, stirring frequently, for about 2 minutes or until the rice is opaque. Stir in the wine and cook, stirring frequently, until all moisture is absorbed.

3. In a separate large saucepan, combine the seafood or chicken stock and the vegetable stock; bring to a simmer over medium-low heat.

4. Fold the orach into the rice and cook, stirring, until the rice turns pink. Season with the salt and pepper.

5. Add the hot stock to the rice mixture in ¾-cup portions. Stir after each addition, until the liquid is absorbed, before adding more stock. Continue to add and stir the hot stock into rice until the rice is cooked and the stock is completely used. Season to taste with salt and pepper.

6. Garnish with Parmesan cheese before serving.

Oregano

Origanum spp.

Lamiaceae

Origanum is in the mint family, which includes important herbs useful for their flavors, fragrances, and medicinal properties. Eurasia is the home of plants in the *Origanum* genus. In the Victorian language of flowers, both marjoram and oregano signify joy and happiness.

Description—Culture—Growing

Origanum species are perennials with varying degrees of hardiness throughout the United States. Many are labeled as tender, meaning they may or may not survive a winter depending on how well they are mulched, temperatures, and snow cover. Oregano as a group is somewhat confusing as there are many species to grow, some of which are purely ornamental. My advice is to let your nose lead you to a good cooking oregano when purchasing it. The tall, purple-flowered marjoram *O. vulgare* subsp. *vulgare* is often sold as culinary oregano. But it tends to be somewhat weedy and does not have a pleasant flavor; this is one to avoid.

Propagation

The preferred method of propagation for *Origanum* is to root cuttings from a stock (mother) plant. In late February or early March take cuttings from new growth. Generally, these cuttings are rooted within two weeks and will be later transplanted into three-inch pots to develop a good root system before moving outside.

Uses

Oregano dries easily and stores well in a cool, dark place. Dry sprigs on screens or hang them upside down in bunches. Just strip the dried leaves from the stems and store in a glass jar for use later. I prefer to use a mortar and pestle to grind this dried herb just before I use it to preserve the oils in the leaves as long as possible.

Oreganos to Grow

DWARF OREGANO

O. microphyllum

The genus *Origanum* is represented in Crete by five species: *O. dictamnus, O. calcaratum, O. microphyllum, O. onites*, and *O. vulgare* subsp. *hirtum*. It had been several years since I had grown *O. onites*, Cretan oregano, and I mail-ordered a plant. When it arrived, it didn't look like what I had ordered, but I potted it up and grew it anyway. After corresponding and sending photos to Rodo and Nikos at Tofillo (an herbal tea company in Chania, Crete), they believed that my plant looked very close to *O. microphyllum*, or dwarf oregano. They wrote, "Indeed as far as we can see from the pictures that you sent us your *Origanum* is very very close to our *O. microphyllum*. *O. microphyllum* is endemic in Crete and we use it as an herbal tea specialty in combination with our Cretan mountain tea! In Crete you will find it on the mountains of our island and indeed it is a very beautiful plant despite its very small leaves and flowers. Its scent is strong and characteristic at our mountains! We sent you a couple of pictures of how it looks wild at its natural environment." In Crete it grows on rocky ground, in rock crevices, and in limestone. It flowers from June to September. Dwarf oregano is very

O. *microphyllum* is found on the mountains of the island of Crete.

beautiful, and I will use it in my teas as well. I followed up with correspondence to the grower and he was happy to know its correct identification and is changing the name. The tiny, aromatic, blue-green leaves are held on rigid wiry stems on which purple flowers bloom in midsummer. It is a fabulous little plant for the deck—it loves the sun and survives with little attention.

'HILLTOP HERB FARM' OREGANO

O. x *majoricum* 'Hilltop Herb Farm'

One of the best oreganos to grow and use for its oregano flavor is the cultivar 'Hilltop Herb Farm'. Once plants have become established in the garden, they require little water except in times of drought. 'Hilltop Herb Farm' oregano grows well in a container or raised planter. Another way to grow it is in a strawberry jar; you can keep it near the kitchen door for easy gathering. In the garden it grows to eighteen inches tall. It does well with other herbs and is not finicky at all. In cold climates it is easy to overwinter 'Hilltop Herb Farm' oregano indoors in direct sunlight in a south-facing window. I have to do this and, surprisingly, the plants do very well in this location during the winter months, but they are very anxious to get outdoors in early May. On several occasions, plants have been overwintered outdoors in Minnesota; mulch is extra insurance and late October or early November is the time to put straw mulch or leaves on this oregano.

Madalene Hill always advised to add 'Hilltop Herb Farm' oregano to sauces, soups, and stews. Combine the branches with shallots, garlic, and onions in a bed underneath meat such as a turkey or a leg of lamb, and baste with wine. By keeping the herbs *under* the meat instead of on top, they will flavor it without burning. She also used this oregano in seasoning mixtures, spaghetti sauces with tomatoes, sausages, vegetables, mushrooms, and in vinegar. 'Hilltop Herb Farm' oregano is used for its aromatic leaves, either fresh or dried.

Rex Talbert's 'Hilltop Herb Farm' Oregano

In 1968, Rex Talbert, HSA (Herb Society of America), herb nomenclature and *Thymus* expert, gave Madalene Hill, HSA, herb expert and grower in Houston, Texas, a special oregano. They both agreed that the plant had an unusual aroma and taste. Madalene grew it as an "unidentified" oregano and sold it as Rex's oregano for several years until Dr. Arthur Tucker, HSA, taxonomist, and emeritus professor, identified it as *Origanum x majoricum*. In 1983 a tornado destroyed all of Madalene's plants and records including those of this oregano. Nearly seventeen years later Madalene's plant came back to her from Elizabeth Winston, who gifted her more plants of this cultivar. This is how plants continue to survive when they are shared with friends. Madalene was very happy to have it back in her possession, and she said she now has the progeny of the plant she received in that small, three-inch pot that Rex originally gave her in 1968. 'Hilltop Herb Farm' oregano can be described as a hybrid of two plants: sweet marjoram, *O. majorana* (for its fragrance), and wild marjoram, *O. vulgare* subsp. *virens* (for its hardiness). The plant leaves are a darker green with a slight bite of carvacrol giving it a hint of oregano. According to Rex, 'Hilltop Herb Farm' is the best in the trade for its flavor and scent.

Note: It is well worth your time to search for this oregano for your garden or for containers so you can enjoy in your kitchen.

Theresa's Seasoning Blend

In this seasoning use dried, rubbed herbs, not ones that are totally ground. It's a tasty mixture of herbs to add to omelets, butter, mustard, vegetables, chicken, and fish.

2 tablespoons chopped parsley

2 tablespoons chopped basil

2 tablespoons oregano

1 tablespoon thyme

1 tablespoon rosemary

1 tablespoon garlic

1 teaspoon lovage

⅛ teaspoon cayenne

1. Blend the parsley, basil, oregano, thyme, rosemary, garlic, lovage, and cayenne together in a small bowl. Transfer to a small glass jar with a lid.

2. Store in a cool, dark cupboard.

135

Oregano

O. 'Kent Beauty'

'Kent Beauty' oregano is a spectacular plant when it's in flower. It was found as a chance seedling in 1978 at Washfield Nursery, Kent, England. Its parents were most likely *O. rotundifolium* and *O. scabrum*. The species *O. rotundifolium* was introduced into cultivation by the British plant collectors Cheese, Mitchell, and Watson after a collecting expedition to Turkey in 1967. Watson is responsible for making many attractive species available for general cultivation and has contributed significantly to the understanding of alpine plants. This species occurs in northeastern Turkey and the adjacent Caucasus Mountains in calcareous and non-calcareous areas. It can be grown in a rock garden if the site is well drained, or it can be grown it in a container. 'Kent Beauty' is propagated by softwood cuttings in early spring. The flowers appear at the tips of six- to eight-inch-long stems. Its rose-stained bracts will soften the edges of any wall or border. It is grown as an ornamental; other *Origanum* species have better flavor for culinary purposes. In milder winters I had this oregano overwinter in the garden. The cut stems can be dried for use in herbal wreaths and herbal craft projects.

LIBANOTICUM OREGANO

O. libanoticum

For many years *O. libanoticum* has been grown in gardens along the Pacific Coast from British Columbia to Southern California. It is a native of the Lebanon Mountains, where it has been found in several places.

O. libanoticum for a number of years was wrongly named as *O. pulchellum* and was correctly identified by Dr. Arthur Tucker. It is a beautiful plant, and I can attest to that after growing it for a number of years in my rock garden and in containers on the deck. The flowers droop over the edge of the container as the flower bracts open and extend two to four inches. As you can see in the photo pink flowers begin peeking out of the bracts for a spectacular show. It is a plant that is the envy of those who see it. In mild winters it survives in the rock garden in my northern climate but most of the time it does not. It is a staple plant in my basement for the winter months. It is easily grown from cuttings in mid-March.

O. syriacum subsp. *syriacum*

Za'atar is an herb plant but it's also the name used to designate a condiment for food.

As a condiment: From Lebanon, Sicilian sumac (*Rhus coriaria*), with its crimson red fruits, is a component of the popular spice mixture called "za'atar."

As a plant: A lesser known oregano is *O. syriacum*, called Syrian oregano or za'atar, which has a sharp flavor. The plant bears foliage with a strong camphor taste; its oils are said to inhibit bacterial growth. This plant is a frost-tender perennial herb with highly aromatic foliage. In its native land, za'atar is described as growing two and one-half feet tall but in northern climates an average garden height is twelve inches. It has wiry square stems and small downy leaves, while white flowers grow in dense clusters at the top of the stems. Honeybees are attracted to their fragrant blossoms. The herb za'atar is easily grown from seed or cuttings. This oregano is a popular herb (fresh or dried) for seasoning soups, sauces, salads, stuffings, stews, roasts, vegetables, and meats. The za'atar condiment, which is exceedingly popular in the Middle East, is often baked into the crust of pita.

Hassan Kaakani's Za'atar

"My homeland is Beirut, Lebanon, and now my home is in Minnesota with my wife, Susan. I grew up eating za'atar on pita bread with my family. The dried mixture is blended with olive oil, and contains dried sumac, oregano, thyme, sometimes marjoram, salt, and roasted sesame seeds. We also eat it fresh, and this is called *za'atar akhdar*, which means "green za'atar" in Arabic. This is also combined with oil, and occasionally chopped onions, and eaten with pita bread. It is enjoyed by the entire family and is not used as a spice blend for cooking in Lebanon. An option in Beirut is to mix your za'atar with oil, take it to the local bakery, and have them make pitas with za'atar, which is called *M'naeesh*. It is a very popular breakfast food, but [it's] rarely eaten at other meals. In the Middle East many homemakers buy the individual spices and mix their own za'atar. This is often done because it assures the sesame seeds will be fresh, as they age faster than the dry herbs. Sumac is used in a very traditional Lebanese bread salad called Fattoush. This salad is usually used for breaking the fast during Ramadan. My father always like to use purslane leaves for his Fattoush, but it's usually seen with romaine in restaurants."

Counterclockwise from the top are shown za'atar mix, Sicilian sumac, dried herbs, and pita bread with za'atar.

Papalo and Pepicha

Porophyllum spp.

Asteraceae

Porophyllum is a tropical and subtropical genus of about thirty species. It is native to the Western Hemisphere, occurring in southern Nevada, California, southwestern Texas, and Arizona south to southern Peru, northern Argentina, and southern Brazil. The word *Porophyllum* is derived from the Greek words *porus*, meaning "pore or passage," and *phyllon*, meaning "leaf." Inhabitants of the southwestern United States and Mexico call the species *hierba del venado* or *yerba del menado*, meaning "deer weed." It seems that wildlife and cattle enjoy several species of *Porophyllum*.

Porophyllum Species to Grow

PAPALO

Porophyllum rudale subsp. *macrocephalum*

Papalo's native habitat is from Arizona and Texas, through Mexico and Central America, to South America. It grows wild in pastures, on hillsides in Mexico, in ravines, and in other brushlands. Leaves are one to two and one-half inches long, and the plants have grown as tall as three feet in my garden. Papalo is sold as a green vegetable in the markets in Veracruz, Mexico. The leaves are somewhat unique in that oil glands occur at each wavy leaf notch and are scattered over its surface; these pores can be seen with the naked eye. The unique flowers of papalo emerge as an elongated capsule and, when fully

opened, look similar to dandelion seed heads as slowly the seeds disperse. Ideally, plant papalo in full sun, but it will also take light shade in the late afternoon. The nearly round leaves are slightly notched, light green in color, and feel velvety to the touch. Cilantro lovers usually don't stray from cilantro, but if you do, try this herb. It is easily grown from seed sown directly into the garden once the ground has warmed up in the spring. Where papalo grows wild, a glass of water with a few branches of papalo is a staple on dinner tables in restaurants, along with salsa and hot chile peppers for

guests to add to their dishes. Its complex flavor is excellent in fresh tomato salsa and in smoky chipotle pepper salsa. Not only is papalo flavorful in foods, but it is an ornamental plant in the garden too. I have a friend who despises cilantro but who will tolerate papalo. Papalo shares similar chemicals with cilantro but it is distinctly different and not identical. If you don't care for cilantro perhaps you may enjoy the flavor of papalo.

Herbed Tapenade

Papalo is a cilantro-mimicking herb from Mexico and South America that adds a piquant flavor to dishes. Use tender leaves from a few sprigs of it along with a mix of other fresh green herbs such as thyme, oregano, rosemary, lemon balm, or sage in this tapenade.

2 cloves garlic

1 fresh or dried cayenne pepper

1 cup pitted black or green olives

½ cup fresh chopped herbs such as thyme, oregano, rosemary, lemon balm, and sage

⅓ cup salted pine nuts or sunflower seeds

1 teaspoon ground cumin

juice of ½ lime

¼ cup extra-virgin hemp or olive oil

1. Combine the garlic and cayenne pepper in the bowl of a food processor. Pulse for 30 seconds or until it is chopped.

2. Add the olives, herbs, pine nuts or sunflower seeds, cumin, and lime juice. Process for 30 seconds.

3. With the motor running, slowly add the hemp or olive oil through the opening in the lid. Keep adding the oil until the mixture is soft and spreadable (you may not need all of the oil).

143

Papalo and Pepicha

PEPICHA

Porophyllum linaria

Pepicha, sometimes called chepiche, is well known in Oaxaca, Mexico, as a native aromatic herb with a pungent flavor similar to that of papalo. This plant is different in that it has thin, stringy leaves that are grayish green in color. Flowerheads, which are later followed by seeds, are non-showy, small, and one-half inch. It will reseed and come back year after year. I planted it once, and it always returns in the same spot by the bird bath. It is never invasive; it's just there. Coarsely chop pepicha and add to mixed salads, fresh salsas, and deviled eggs. Pepicha also pairs well with grain-based salads such as tabbouleh, mujaddara (bulgur wheat), tapenade, or potato salad. Add pepicha at the end of the cooking process to maintain its flavor. Pepicha can act as a palate cleanser after meals. Pepicha's flavor and aroma have hints of pine, citrus, and mint, and it's an herb with a strong, clean fragrance that's used both traditionally and in Mexican cuisine.

Porterweed

Stachytarpheta spp.

Verbenaceae

Porterweed is a perennial herb with opposite, simple leaves that are sometimes dentate to serrate. The genus is widely distributed in tropical and subtropical America, Asia, and Africa. *Stachytarpheta jamaicensis* was first recorded in Hawaii in 1913 where it is commonly found at 1,400-foot elevations in dry, disturbed places. In Australia, all *Stachytarpheta* species are naturalized, and most of them are cultivated as ornamental or hedge plants.

Description—Culture—Growing

When porterweed is in bloom only a few flowers of the same spike are open simultaneously. They are ephemerous, expanding in the early morning and falling off in the afternoon of the same day. After a spike or a flower has been separated from the plant the corolla is shed within a few minutes. If a cut stem is placed in water new flowers will open the following morning. Porterweed plants are easily cared for whether they are planted in containers or the garden. Full sun or at least afternoon sun is important for the plant to flower. To produce a bountiful crop of flowers it is advisable to purchase a fertilizer with a higher phosphorus ratio. Early spring is an opportune time to transplant porterweed. Remove the plant, trim about one inch of roots around the soil ball (outside and bottom), place the plant back into the container, and add new soil around the sides and bottom. Just as important is to cut the growth of the stems back approximately one-third. What you have just done is encourage growth in the roots and the top.

Propagation

Vegetative propagation is the best way to increase the number of porterweed plants. Take cuttings from fresh new growth occurring in early spring.

Uses

The two varieties listed here are both favorites of hummingbirds and butterflies. As soon as the first flowers emerge you can sit back and enjoy nature at work.

Porterweeds to Grow

BLUE PORTERWEED

S. jamaicensis

Blue porterweed is a small shrub bearing small blue flowers with a white throat that continue all summer on whiplike spikes. It is distinguished by its low habit, opposite

leaves, and serrate leaf margins. The elongated thick spikes are embedded with flowers along the stem. According to Dr. Harold N. Moldenke, New Jersey, a well-known plant systematist, editor of *Phytologia*, and a curator at the New York Botanica Garden, "The juice of the leaves, roots, or even the entire plant is used in many countries as a tonic, emetic, expectorant, ... stimulant, ... purgative, and cooling agent. It is used locally in various parts of its range in the treatment of headaches, earaches....In Cuba the juice is used as a bath to treat skin diseases. It is also known as blue snakeweed, Jamaica vervain, verbena azul, Jamaica false vervain, and vervain."

RED PORTERWEED

S. mutabilis

Red porterweed is a native to South America and is naturalized in Australia in the tropical areas of northeastern Queensland. According to Dr. Harold N. Moldenke, "This species is rather widespread in the American tropics from Mexico and Cuba, through Central America, and the West Indies to northern South America, and Central Brazil….it is widely cultivated in Europe (since 1801), America, and Australia." The plant is bushy and in early summer fills with stems that eventually bloom the rest of the summer. In the summer I grow the red porterweed on the deck, and it is eighteen inches by eighteen inches in the container. It begins flowering the first week of July and will continue until frost in early October. The flowers are a bright red, approximately one-quarter inch in diameter, and attached to the elongated stems. It's amazing to watch the hummingbirds gracefully dip their bills into the flowers.

Rosemary, 'Shady Acres'

Rosmarinus officinalis 'Shady Acres'

Lamiaceae

Rosemary is an aromatic evergreen perennial shrub native in the
hills along the Mediterranean that was eventually introduced into
many parts of Europe. On a recent visit to Gruene, Texas, and its
neighboring towns, I saw four-foot-tall rosemary plants planted
at the entrance to many small shops. It was a welcome sight for
a Minnesota visitor to see these as many flower in February. In
the language of flowers, rosemary is best known for its meaning
of remembrance, friendship, loyalty, and fidelity. Mrs. M. Grieve,
author of *A Modern Herbal* (1931) writes, "...the Ancients were well
acquainted with the shrub, which had a reputation for strengthening
the memory. On this account it became the emblem of fidelity for
lovers. It holds a special position among herbs from the symbolism
attached to it. Not only was rosemary used at weddings, but it was
also used at funerals, for decking churches and banquet halls at
festivals, as incense in religious ceremonies, and in magical spells."
Rosemary was dried for potpourri, strewn for fragrance, and burned
as an incense substitute in churches many years ago.

The following historical description was written by Dr. Arthur
Tucker in the *Encyclopedia of Herbs*, "Rosemary symbolizes
remembrance, and for good reason. After working with rosemary
plants for any length of time or even brushing against them, its piney
fragrance clings with special fondness to wool, hair, and human skin.
Its fragrance invokes images of fresh-roasted lamb on skewers of
rosemary branches prepared over a campfire on a gravelly beach
with the Mediterranean Sea breaking in the background.

Rosmarinus species are often found clinging to sea cliffs. The common name is aptly derived from the Latin words *ros*, meaning 'dew' or 'spray,' and *marinus*, meaning 'sea.' The specific epithet, *officinalis*, means 'of the shops,' or medicinal. Its narrow leaves are tightly arranged along branches, giving it, along with its piney scent, the general appearance of a conifer. The brilliant blue flowers, which can appear almost any time of the year depending upon the cultivar, supposedly assumed their color when the Virgin Mary draped her cloak upon a plant to dry on her flight into Egypt."

Description—Culture—Growing

I cannot imagine *not* having rosemary to clip for culinary use, so I keep it close to the kitchen door in full sun. It has one-inch-long, dark green leaves and strong, upright growth habit with deep blue flowers that appear sporadically in winter. In my rural Minnesota garden, it is a tender perennial that I grow in a container in summer; each fall I bring it into my home. Growing rosemary indoors can be a challenge. One tip is when you water the plant, water it thoroughly, and then let it dry out before watering again. The cooler the temperature is indoors, the happier rosemary will be—even down to 40 to 50 degrees F. Position it in a south- or west-facing exposure for the best growth. Rosemary does well in containers in potting soil with good drainage. Transplant rosemary once a year, preferably in spring before new growth starts. When the plant finally gets too big to move to a larger pot, remove it from the pot, shave about two inches of roots and soil from the outside edges and bottom, and transplant it back into the same pot. When doing this type of invasive pruning make sure to prune the top of the plant by one-third to compensate for the root pruning. This stimulates new root and top growth. Use an organic fertilizer twice monthly in the summer.

Theresa Mieseler's 'Shady Acres' Rosemary

In 1999 I introduced 'Shady Acres' rosemary. It struck me as having an excellent fragrance that would be good to cook with as well as strong, upright growth as a bush rosemary. After a number of years of growing rosemary seedlings, I selected this particular specimen because it really appealed to me. In February 2001 I asked Dr. Arthur O. Tucker, Department of Agriculture & Natural Resources, Delaware State University, to perform an analysis of 'Shady Acres' rosemary. He graciously said he would, and I mailed a box of rosemary stems to him.

Essential oil analysis of 'Shady Acres' rosemary by Dr. Arthur Tucker

constituent=%
alpha-pinene=26.46
camphene=5.09
beta-pinenel1e=4.55
myrcene=1.87
beta-phellandrene=0.05
1,8-cineole=23.11
gamma-terpinene=2.30
p-cymene=1.05
terpinolene=1.74
alpha-p-dimethyl-styrene=0.08
trans-sabinene hydrate=0.38
camphor=4.62
linalool=1.16
cis-sabinene hydrate=0.52

isopinocamphone=1.16
pinocarvone=1.21
bornyl acetate=0.85
terpinen-4-ol=1.64
(E)-beta-caryophyllene=1.45
isoborneol=1.29
borneol=1.85
verbenone=6.93
geranyl acetate=0.40
citronellol=0.21
trans-carveol=0.06
geraniol=2.94
caryophyllene oxide=0.10
methyl eugenol=0.28

Rex Talbert's Evaluation of Dr. Arthur Tucker's Analysis

"The data that Arthur sent you indicates that indeed our noses were correct and your 'Shady Acres' rosemary would make an excellent cooking rosemary. The camphor and camphene concentrations are low, producing a less objectionable flavor and toxicity. The alpha pinene (pine scent), geraniol (rose scent), bornyl acetate, isoborneol & borneol (rosemary scents) make for a pleasant and recognizable rosemary fragrance. The relatively high verbenone is valued by herbal medicinal practitioners and is comparatively rare."

Propagation

Most rosemary plants are cultivars or clones, which are propagated only by cuttings. When rosemary is grown from seed there is plant variation and low germination, but with cuttings the plants are always as uniform as the stock (mother) plant. I have found the best time of year to take cuttings is in February. Stems from new growth are taken about two and one-half inches long. Snip off the bottom leaves, dip the bottom one-quarter inch of the cutting into a weak rooting hormone powder, and stick these cuttings into a container filled with equal measures of peat moss and perlite. Bottom heat speeds the rooting process. Spray a light mist of water on sunny days. After the cuttings root, in fourteen to twenty-one days, transplant them into three-inch pots and pinch the top terminal bud to encourage branching. Rosemary is not a difficult plant to propagate; oftentimes roots will develop in a glass of water on a sunny windowsill.

Uses

Rosemary is preserved best by drying the leaves and stems, which preserves the essential oils for cooking and keeps for a long time. I cut rosemary stems, use a rubber band to keep the stems together, and hang the bunch from a kitchen cupboard door handle where it will dry in seven to ten days. You can also strip the leaves; place the stems on a paper towel-lined cookie sheet to dry. When the stems are brittle I strip the leaves and store them in a glass bottle in my cupboard. I prefer using glass because the essential oils can be absorbed by plastic containers. When I'm ready to use the rosemary, I grind it using a mortar and pestle or a mini food processor. A roast chicken is not complete without rosemary—fresh or dried, I add it to a small amount of olive oil, tuck it under the skin of the chicken, and place the chicken on a grill or in the oven. Add rosemary to potatoes, lamb, salmon, eggs, butters, mustard, drinks, and pizza dough.

Grilled Rosemary Chicken

You may find it takes a little more time, or a little less time, to cook the chicken; just *don't* overcook it.

½ cup extra-virgin olive oil

2 cloves garlic, finely chopped

2 tablespoons fresh lemon juice

2 tablespoons balsamic or red wine vinegar

1½ tablespoons Worcestershire sauce

1 tablespoon dried rosemary or 2 tablespoons fresh rosemary

2 teaspoons Dijon mustard

1 teaspoon dried basil or 1 tablespoon fresh basil

1 teaspoon crushed red pepper flakes

1 teaspoon sea salt

2 frying chickens, cut into serving pieces

1. Combine the olive oil, garlic, lemon juice, vinegar, Worcestershire sauce, rosemary, mustard, basil, red pepper, and salt in a large bowl. Stir to mix well.

2. Place the chicken pieces into a large plastic bag. Pour the marinade over the chicken. Seal the bag and refrigerate 2 to 3 hours.

Bring the chicken to room temperature and grill on an outdoor grill or broil the chicken on the top rack in the oven, turning after about 15 minutes per side. Cook until done (the juices will run clear) or when a meat thermometer registers 165 degrees F.

153

Rosemary, 'Shady Acres'

Sage

Salvia spp.

Lamiaceae

Salvus was a name used by the Romans for *Salvia* and it meant "good health." *Salvia* encompasses a large genus of plants. Many are flavorful to use in the kitchen for a wide variety of foods. In the garden the selection of beautiful flower colors and fragrances, leaf textures, and plant sizes is almost endless. Unfortunately, many of the beautiful cultivars are not hardy in northern climates and are grown as annuals. Visit www.robinssalvias.com for a lovely pictorial album as well as correctly identified varieties. One only has to look through the plant catalogs to see the direction the industry is headed. It is exciting to browse and try something new!

Description—Culture—Growing

Salvias are some of the showiest plants for color in containers, mixed borders, and gardens whether they are annual or perennial. Butterflies and hummingbirds love them. Some of the following sages are for cooking, some are for wildlife, and some are just for their beauty. Full sun and a well-drained soil are requirements for nearly all species, especially garden sage. If not, it will begin to wilt. You may think it needs more water, but, in fact, it does not have enough drainage.

Propagation

Salvia officinalis, garden sage, is easily grown from seed. The *Salvia* as described here require vegetative propagation by means of cuttings or sometimes root division. Search the internet for *Salvia* specialists either near you or accessible by mail order. Adding several varieties will surely be a highlight to your garden. Some varieties will perform well in different areas of the country better than others. It is well worth the time to research the plants suited for your zone.

Uses

If your pleasure is culinary, landscape use, fragrance, medicinal herbal alternatives, or perhaps natural beauty products there is a wide range of *Salvia* from which to choose.

Sages to Grow

CLEVELAND SAGE

S. clevelandii

Cleveland sage impressed me some forty years ago when I was a young herb gardener. Plants and people associations are important to me, whether it's working in the garden or with plants on my deck; they're a reminder to me of the plants I received from friends. Such is the story of Cleveland sage. This is just one example of the people and plant associations that happen time after time. Bernice Anderson introduced me to herbs, and one of my first herbs was Cleveland sage. It was the fragrance of this plant that captured my senses. It is heavenly (perhaps not at all how experts would define scents), and I'll never forget the first time I was with Bernice and inhaled the aroma of this sage. I don't know of any other plant to which to compare its scent; some say it is similar to rose potpourri. *S. clevelandii* is easy to grow but, unfortunately, it is not winter-hardy in northern climates. It is a small shrub that grows three to five feet in its native area with pebbly-looking leaves. My plant only reaches a height of thirty inches and flowers with spikes rising well above the leaves

in summer. One to three whorls of blue-violet blossoms open in stages, and the hummingbirds and bees dip into them as soon as possible. I prefer to grow it in a container and bring it indoors for the winter where it does very well until it can return outdoors in mid-May. It grows in full sun and will tolerate morning shade with afternoon sun. Pruning in the spring keeps it in a nice form; otherwise, it gets a little rangy. There is a wide range of plants called *S. clevelandii* that are hybrids and cross with other *Salvia* in California. Perhaps it is impossible to find the original *S. clevelandii* anymore, but the hybrids are certainly well worth growing. *S. clevelandii* was named in 1874 by Harvard's Asa Gray, the botanist (1810–1888) after Daniel Cleveland (1838–1929). Today most plants available are actually hybrids of *S. clevelandii* x *S. leucophylla*.

GREEK SAGE

S. fruticosa

S. fruticosa is endemic to the Mediterranean region, the southern Balkans, southern Italy, Turkey, and Libya, and can be found growing in open shrubby areas. The plant's flowers are variable, meaning they can be pale blue, pink, or white, and the foliage has variable shapes. It grows in full sun but will take partial shade and is a tender perennial in frost areas. Propagation is from seed or by cuttings. *S. fruticosa* is laden with history and lore. It has probably been utilized since 1400 BC and is illustrated in the "blue bird fresco" in the House of Frescoes, Knossos, located southeast of the city of Iraklion, Crete. Greek sage works well as an incense, with a fragrance similar to that of the white sage, *S. apiana*. In medieval times, *S. fruticosa* was considered a "panacea," or a cure-all, and was cultivated in monastery gardens. Dr. Arthur Tucker wrote, "The plant most associated with the American Thanksgiving is hidden in our stuffing—sage. In times far removed from the historic record, sage was probably originally incorporated into food as a preservative, but today nobody can imagine sausage or stuffing without it. We utilize two species of *Salvia* as culinary sage, and both originated in Europe, *S. officinalis* from northern Europe, and *S. fruticosa* from the shores of the Mediterranean." A tea is made from the dried leaves and is sold in cafés in Greece under the name "faskomilo" with a similar herbal tea made in Istanbul, Turkey. In 1989, Simon, Chadwick, and Craker reported that fifty percent of the culinary sage imported into the United States as common sage is *S. fruticosa*; it's interesting what we don't know.

'MULBERRY JAM' SAGE

S. 'Mulberry Jam'

'Mulberry Jam' is a hybrid of *S. involucrata* that was discovered in the garden of Betsy Clebsch in California. In my garden it is a tender perennial that reaches four feet tall with flowers appearing in mid-July until the first frost. The mauve calyces with two-inch, rose-colored tubular flowers are shining stars. 'Mulberry Jam' prefers to be in full sun, sheltered from strong winds. It is a very showy sage that is well worth planting each year, especially for the hummingbirds. It is not edible.

Betsy Clebsch's 'Mulberry Jam' Sage

"*Salvia involucrata* is known for its propensity to cross freely with other *Salvia* species. Hybrids have occurred at the University of California Botanical Garden, Berkeley. These plants show hybrid vigor, attaining approximately six feet in height, and have a long blooming period. In the summer of 1991, a four-foot-tall spontaneous hybrid of *S. involucrata* bloomed in my garden. Smaller in stature than the species, this hybrid is well suited for a small garden and is considered a well-behaved addition to the summer and autumn borders. The plant holds itself upright because its stems are thin and woody. It was introduced [commercially] in the fall of 1995, and I've known it as *Salvia involucrata* 'Mulberry Jam'. 'Mulberry Jam' sage begins to flower in mid- to late summer and continues until frost. If you remove old inflorescences throughout the blooming season, the tall flowering stems will stay erect. Cuttings taken in late summer or early autumn will root rapidly."

'WILD WATERMELON' LITTLELEAF SAGE

S. microphylla 'Wild Watermelon'

'Wild Watermelon' sage is originally from Mexico and is a beautiful specimen in the garden. It is a very fast-growing plant, with freely produced, medium-sized, dark pink with white-marked flower throats, and attractive foliage. It grows to two feet in northern climates. 'Wild Watermelon' sage prefers a location in full sun and soil with good drainage. Seeds of this variety appear to come true, but there is no guarantee. Therefore, cuttings are the best method to maintain identical plants. It is vigorous, very floriferous, and the flowers are larger than other forms of *S. microphylla*. It has no known herbal or medicinal use. It is just grown for its beauty, and to attract butterflies and hummingbirds. It was collected by Don Mahoney at an elevation of 7,000 to 8,500 feet on Mt. Cerro El Potosí, which is located in the Sierra Madre Oriental mountain range in northeast Mexico. Mt. Cerro El Potosí is about fifty miles south of Monterrey in the state of Nuevo Leon.

Robin Middleton, England

Robin was helpful assisting me with *Salvia* questions and identification. He wrote this about his life and gardening with *Salvia*, "As for myself, my interest in *Salvia* began twenty-five years ago when I visited a friend's garden who had a collection of *Salvia*. I was amazed at some of the colors and started to visit specialist nurseries. I gradually built up a large collection. Since the internet, I have contacts all over the world, we visit each other, and exchange seeds and plants. I am not so young now, so I am sadly cutting down on my collection, to make life a bit easier! *Salvia* are native to all continents except Australasia, though there are some exciting collections there." Visit the website at: http://www.robinssalvias.com/index.html.

Salad Burnet, 'Tanna'

Sanguisorba 'Tanna'

Rosaceae

The genus *Sanguisorba* is native to Europe and Asia, and it came to America with the Pilgrims. It seems unlikely but salad burnet is a member of the rose family. The genus name *Sanguisorba* comes from the Latin words meaning "blood" and "drink up" in reference to the herb's traditional property as a styptic (to stop bleeding). Colonial soldiers in the American Revolutionary War (1775–1783) are said to have drunk salad burnet tea before engaging in skirmishes to prevent bleeding should they be wounded. 'Tanna' is a lovely, compact salad burnet cultivar from Japan. While researching this plant, I came across the name and work of Piet Oudolf, a Dutch garden designer renowned for his work in Europe, Canada, and the United States. In June 2018, I wrote to Mr. Oudolf asking him about the origin of this burnet, and he wrote back stating, "In the early eighties we ordered seed from a Japanese seed company. This seed was called *Sanguisorba* 'Tanna'. We kept it under this name. More, we don't know about the origin."

Description—Culture—Growing

'Tanna' salad burnet is a small, decorative herb growing two inches high by eight inches wide with an abundance of dense, oblong, burgundy flowers that rise well above the plant. It is a magnet for bees and butterflies. Its bright green foliage is serrated with red-margined edges. When new growth emerges, it is folded; as it matures, it unfolds. The long-lasting flowers are stunning as is the pinnate foliage that keeps it shape throughout the growing season. It is well suited for rock gardens, fairy gardens, or containers with its mounds of fernlike leaves. It likes full sun or partial shade in the garden. A word of warning: I photographed this plant in flower. The next day I went back to take more shots, and I discovered a local bunny had been having what I assumed was its entrée. The flowers were completely gone.

Propagation

Propagate 'Tanna' by seeds or root division in early spring.

Uses

'Tanna' is so small and compact that it does not produce abundant foliage, making it useful as an ornamental herb rather than a culinary one. Therefore, I recommend using the species of salad burnet for culinary purposes. Its abundant leaves should be used directly from the garden or container as freshly cut; drying the leaves doesn't do justice to this plant. Cultivated since the Middle Ages, the cucumber-flavored foliage has been a welcome addition to salads, herbal vinegars, and combined with other herbs in butters, drinks, fish sauces, soups, cream cheese, and as a garnish.

Scented Geraniums

Pelargonium spp.

Geraniaceae

South Africa is the home to many of the scented geraniums that were discovered in the early 1600s. In 1632 they were brought to England and soon gained popularity in the perfume industry in France. By 1800 geranium oils distilled at Grasse, France, began to replace the more expensive rose oils. Great plantations of scented geraniums were developed by the British in colonial Kenya. Before the American Revolution, they were brought to the United States where they became popular in Colonial days. Some of these plants were used in cooking by 1818. Helen Van Pelt Wilson, writing in *The Joy of Geraniums*, suggests there are seven practical groupings of scented geraniums: apple, mint, fruit, lemon, nut, spice, and pungent. Let your nose be your guide!

Description—Culture—Growing

Scented geraniums are perennials that are treated as tender perennials in northern climates. They are a joy to grow, and their fragrance is delightful. Varieties of leaf textures, shapes, fragrances, flower colors, and growth patterns offer endless choices. I have featured three of my favorites, but you don't have to stop there. Scented geraniums can be planted in the garden, ideally near a path so their scent can be enjoyed. They grow best in full sun and like good air circulation. I prefer to grow them in containers where you can show them off to friends who aren't familiar with them by brushing the foliage and letting them inhale the aromas. They flower sporadically during the growing season, and while some are striking and showy, many are just small flowers you may not even

notice. The fragrance is not in the flowers but in the leaves, which release the oils when they are brushed. Water containers only when the surface of the soil feels dry; water it well and let dry out again. Yellow leaves can be the result of too much water or not enough fertilizer. If you're looking ahead to winter them over in the house, they are best grown in pots sunk into the garden or grown in containers on the patio or deck during the summer. It is difficult to transplant them into pots when they are fully mature in the garden; that is why it's best to keep them in containers all season. Indoors they are susceptible to whiteflies and aphids, but these are easily controlled by spraying with insecticidal soap diligently applied every three or four days until the pests are gone.

Propagation

The most common method of increasing your collection of scented geraniums is by cuttings. Always select shoots from new growth that are about three inches long and use a soilless mix for rooting. I have taken cuttings from plants, stored them in a plastic bag in the refrigerator overnight, and then inserted them into the potting mix the next day. Rooting hormone is not needed nor is it recommended. Depending on the variety, rooting takes place in approximately two to two and one-half weeks.

Uses

The versatile scented geraniums can be tucked into the garden between herbs and flowers, grown in hanging baskets, trained as topiaries, or just planted in attractive containers. Not all scented geraniums are tasty; some are best just to sniff and enjoy. Scented geraniums to use in the kitchen are the rose and lemon varieties. I prefer to use fresh leaves (not dried) to flavor sugar and in cookies, sweet desserts, cakes, and jellies. A hint from Rex Talbert about baking pound cakes with scented geraniums: Instead of lining the pan with the leaves, just bake the loaf or cake. When the cake is cool, place it in a plastic bag and add several scented geranium leaves. For two or three days take out the old leaves daily and replace with new ones, keeping the cake in the refrigerator. You will have a nice fresh flavor infused into your cake or loaf. I always use the larger-leaved varieties of scented geraniums as a base in tussie mussies or herb nosegays.

Scented Geraniums to Grow

'CY'S SUNBURST' SCENTED GERANIUM

P. crispum 'Cy's Sunburst'

This is a new compact variety with a refreshing lemon scent. It is a great plant to grow in a container on a tabletop outdoors with Corsican mint or a dwarf thyme as an understory plant. It would be a perfect focal point in a fairy or miniature garden. The leaves are white- and green-edged. In the summer I have it planted in the rock garden where it thrives.

Cy and Louise Hyde's 'Cy's Sunburst' Geranium

"'Cy's Sunburst' geranium came from a mutation of *P. crispum* 'Well Sweep Golden Variegated'. It was cloned and named *P. crispum* 'Cy's Sunburst'. This was soon seen as a new selection, and Cy propagated it from there. The plant is compact and upright with small gold and green leaves. It has smaller leaves than most scented geraniums making it suitable for containers or small pots or trained as a topiary. It stands out in the garden or in a container, and glimmer unlike many of the other variegated scented geraniums. 'Cy's Sunburst' will grow twenty inches tall by ten inches wide. Its citrus smell is as pleasingly fresh as that of its parent."

'MABEL GREY' SCENTED GERANIUM

P. citronellum 'Mabel Grey'

'Mabel Grey' scented geranium was introduced from Kenya in 1960. To describe 'Mabel Gray' is easy: It is the ultimate lemon fragrance and the plant needs only be touched to release its scent. An absolute favorite, this geranium has large, diamond-shaped coarse leaves that release a pleasant lemon scent when you rub them. Rather than shrubby or sprawling, this geranium grows straight up. Potted in containers it will grow to three feet. When it flowers, they are mauve colored with deep veining and are large for scented geraniums. I have planted it in a large pot in the center, with blue heliotrope around the outside of the pot. What a combination of lemon and cherries (from the heliotrope). It is a very difficult plant to propagate of all the scented geraniums; cuttings root sporadically and maybe only 5 percent of the lot will root. It is one to be prized and enjoyed! Add a leaf or two to your favorite tea or whip a clipped leaf into butter with honey and spread it on your morning muffin.

'ROBER'S LEMON ROSE' SCENTED GERANIUM

P. graveolens 'Rober's Lemon Rose'

'Rober's Lemon Rose' is easily distinguishable with its irregularly lobed leaves. It is a tender perennial with upright growth. Since it grows fast, pinch out the terminal buds to maintain its shape. It has soft grey-green leaves with scalloped edges that are deeply tri-lobed. The small, pale pink to mauve flowers have five petals each and are held in clusters on long stems. The upper petals have darker colored feathering on them. The spicy scent is of rose with a hint of a lemon undertone.

Kathleen Gip's Tussie Mussies

"A tussie mussie is a small, tightly gathered, handheld bouquet of herbs and flowers. The tussie is often surrounded by a lace or paper doily and tied with ribbon streamers. The herbs and flowers included in the bouquet express a message from the heart of the giver. This symbolic floral language is called 'floriography.' The unusual name 'tussie mussie' is a Middle English word meaning a 'nosegay, a tuzzy-muzzy, a sweet posy' according Alice Morse Earle in her book *Old Time Gardens* (1901).

"Plant symbolism was common knowledge throughout Europe for centuries, but the language of herbs and flowers reached its height of popularity in the 1800s. In France, the first dictionary of floriography was written in 1819 when a French woman, Louise Cortambert, writing under the pen name Madame Charlotte de la Tour, wrote *Le Language des Fleurs* explaining floral symbolism and the meanings of flowers. A tussie mussie was carried not only to be fashionable, as it's both beautiful and fragrant, but also to speak the floral language. Everyone cherishes the gift of a tussie mussie. They can express love, friendship, speedy recovery, baby blessings, bridal happiness, and thanks."

Herbs to Include in a Tussie Mussie and What They Mean

chamomile .... *all your wishes come true*

rose geranium............ *preference*

lavender...................... *devotion*

marjoram..................... *joy*

peppermint .... *warmth of feeling*

rosemary..................... *remembrance*

sage.............................. *long life, good health*

basil.............................. *love*

sweet cicely................ *gladness*

oregano....................... *spiciness*

lemon geranium .... *tranquility of mind*

thyme........................... *happiness, courage*

rose.............................. *love, beauty*

pansy............................ *happy thoughts*

pinks .... *bonds of affection*

marigold...................... *joy, remembrance*

forget-me-nots.......... *true love*

zinnia............................ *thought of absent friends*

feverfew .... *you light up my life*

burnet........................... *a merry heart*

How to Create a Tussie Mussie

Supplies

Assorted flowers (see "Herbs to Include in a Tussie Mussie and What They Mean" to select the ones you'd like)

herb leaves (scented geranium, lamb's ears, fern leaf tansy, or other large herb leaves)

paper or lace doilies

floral tape

ribbon

colored aluminum foil

rubber band or floral tape

1. Cut and gather the herbs and flowers early in the day to ensure the most fragrant foliage and place them in a small bucket of water. When you're ready to create your tussie mussie, arrange the herbs around a central group of flowers. Frame the arrangement with leaves of scented geranium, lamb's ears, fern leaf tansy, or another large-leaved herb. Secure the bouquet with a rubber band (or floral tape) and trim the stems to four inches. To prevent wilting and maintain freshness longer, immerse the stems in warm water, mist the foliage, and refrigerate for a few hours or overnight. The posy can be put into a tiny vase or wrapped as a nosegay when it's presented.

2. To wrap, dampen a small square of paper towel and wrap around the stems. Squeeze out any excess water and cover the towel completely with the colored foil. Cut a 1-inch X in the center of two 6-inch paper doilies and slip the stems through the X. This stem handle may be wrapped with floral tape and ribbon. Tie two lengths of narrow ribbon in a bow at the base.

3. Include a card explaining the meanings of the herbs and flowers you've used. Tussie mussies wrapped in this way will stay fresh without water. After the fresh bouquet has been enjoyed, it can be dried by hanging it upside down or placing it in a vase without water in a dark, dry, and warm spot.

TUSSIE MUSSIE

Society Garlic, 'Silver Lace'

Tulbaghia violacea 'Silver Lace'

Amaryllidaceae

This unusual plant is in the same family as *Allium* species, but it's not the same genus as *Allium*. However, it smells and tastes like an onion-related plant. It is also known as sweet garlic and Ajo ornamental. It comes from northeastern South Africa where it grows along forest margins and stream banks. It was used for food and medicine by the indigenous Zulu tribes. *Tulbaghia* was named in honor of Ryk Tulbagh (1699–1771), Dutch Governor of the Cape of Good Hope, South Africa. During his time in office (1751–1771) he established the Colony's first library, plus a plant and animal collection in the company's gardens.

Description—Culture—Growing

The upright plants are grasslike and they're well worth a place in the garden or grown in a container. It is showy planted in a rock garden or a fairy container with other herbs. Its decorative, long, narrow grey-green variegated leaves are somewhat fleshy, and when they're bruised they emit a garlic scent. Society garlic tends to grow in a clump and is a perennial in warmer climates. The leaves are approximately eight inches long and one-quarter inch wide with white stripes along their margins. A single plant is four to six inches wide. Plant society garlic in full sun in a location with good drainage. The lilac flowers, up to twenty, are grouped into umbels at the top of the plant. Society garlic flowers in early June for approximately three weeks. To enjoy the scent place containers on the deck and enjoy the sweet scent.

Propagation

It has been written that the plant is propagated from seed but I've not seen seed offered, nor have I tried to germinate seed. When the plant gets large enough, six or more stems, it can easily be divided. Remove the society garlic from the container or the garden, spray the soil from the roots with a garden hose, and carefully pull the bulbs apart. Replant, water, and you have the dividing accomplished. Society garlic is not hardy in areas that get a hard frost.

Uses

The young shoots are sometimes used raw or cooked like garlic chives in food such as salads. I prefer making the following butter recipe, using it fresh, and freezing any leftover amount.

Makes about 1¼ cup

Society Garlic Butter

This is really a triple garlic butter! With just a few simple ingredients and a few minutes time, you can serve up a tasty treat.

¾ cup unsalted butter

2 large cloves garlic, peeled and finely chopped

2 tablespoons chopped fresh garlic chives

¼ cup chopped society garlic leaves

1 tablespoon freshly squeezed lemon juice

1 teaspoon fresh chopped oregano

2 tablespoons extra-virgin olive oil

½ cup ricotta cheese

Combine the butter, garlic, garlic chives, society garlic, lemon juice, oregano, olive oil, and ricotta cheese in a mini food processor and process until well blended. Serve on warm crusty French bread, over pasta or rice, or baste grilled fresh vegetables with it.

Solomon's Seal, Variegated

Polygonatum odoratum 'Variegatum'

Asparagaceae

The perennial species is native over a large area across Europe and Asia, from Portugal in the west to Japan in the east. Most of the time it grows in open coniferous forests, in woodland edges, on shaded slopes, and along streams and rivers. In Minnesota it flourishes in our local woods, in shaded and semi-shaded gardens. The variegated variety is stunning with its striped foliage and white drooping flowers in spring.

Description—Culture—Growing

Variegated Solomon's seal is a versatile plant that will grow prolifically in full sun or shade. It is a sport that has streaky, creamy white margins whose sizes may vary on the plants. Its graceful, arching stems add a striking effect to the garden. I recall the first time I saw this plant was in a slide presentation during a lecture by Dr. Leon Snyder, the first director of the Minnesota Landscape Arboretum. The clumps shown in the slide indicated it was a vigorous grower, and I was so impressed. Years later I purchased my first single stem and now, many years later, it is abundant in my gardens in three- to four-foot-tall clumps in several areas. It is still impressive, with foliage that looks perfect all summer long. The stems are burgundy and the flowers are fragrant with beautiful pendant flowers. It's a great plant to use for filler in fresh bouquets because they will last for days. Leaf color in the fall is yellow. The deer love

the green-leaved Solomon's seal but stay away from the variegated form—how nice of them! It grows thirty inches tall with five-inch by two-inch leaves, but I've not seen it produce a berry or seed. It is especially nice that it forms clumps with stalks, almost like a small forest, that are so thick that few weeds have a chance to survive.

Propagation

In early spring small spikes emerge from the ground. When this happens, it is the time to dig up the shallow-rooted rhizomes and plant them in other areas of the garden. If the clump is large and filled with soil, take a garden hose and spray the soil off the roots, which makes it easy to divide the clump and transplant.

Uses

This perennial offers vivid highlights in shaded areas of borders, woodland gardens, or naturalized areas. It fills in nicely without being aggressive.

Clumps of Solomon's seal are thriving in Theresa's garden.

Sorrel, Bloody Dock

Rumex sanguineus

Polygonaceae

This striking sorrel is native to Asia, Iran, Azerbaijan, Georgia, Denmark, and most of Europe. In its native land it grows in ditches and forests, but now it has escaped gardens and naturalized in areas of the United States and Canada.

Description—Culture—Growing

R. sanguineus is known as bloody dock or red-veined sorrel. It is an herbaceous perennial in the buckwheat family that grows in a rounded clump to eighteen inches tall and as wide. Its decorative foliage is an accent in the garden with its oblong to lance-shaped, medium green leaves that are distinctively veined red to purple. In early summer, tiny star-shaped flowers appear in panicles atop reddish stems. Flowers emerge green and eventually mature to reddish brown; they are then followed by reddish brown fruit. In addition to its ornamental virtues, the young leaves of this plant are edible. In mild climates it remains evergreen, but the leaves die back to the ground in harsh winters, and usually it does not overwinter in northern regions. Bloody dock grows in full sun to partial shade in average to moist soil. It is a low-maintenance plant and requires little care. In August, cut the plant back to the ground. In three to four days there will be a new crop of fresh leaves. Doing this prevents the leaves from getting too bitter.

Propagation

Propagate by seed.

Uses

Bloody dock sorrel is grown in vegetable and herb gardens to harvest its edible young leaves. In addition to its ornamental virtues, the young leaves of this plant add interesting color and a spinachlike taste to salads. Leaves also have a hint of lemony tartness. Use it fresh in salads or blanch the leaves a minute or two in boiling water. When quickly sautéed, the leaves melt into a purée that, with a little butter and cream, make a tasty sauce for fish or vegetables. Sorrel cream is a perfect sauce for poached eggs or eggs Benedict too.

Makes 2 servings

Arugula and Red Sorrel Salad

This is such a bright mix! All you have to do is top it simply with the dressing. This red-veined sorrel is pretty, adds zest, and imparts a lemony flavor.

1 cup red-veined sorrel strips

1 cup arugula leaves

3 to 4 sprigs Italian parsley

½ avocado, peeled, pitted, and thinly sliced

½ orange, peeled, and thinly sliced, discarding any seeds

¼ cup crumbled feta cheese

Dressing

2 teaspoons apple cider vinegar

1 or 2 dashes sherry vinegar

1 tablespoon extra-virgin olive oil

1 tablespoon honey

¼ teaspoon dry mustard

Sea salt and freshly cracked black pepper

1. In a medium-sized bowl, combine the sorrel, arugula, and parsley. Toss to mix well and divide the greens between 2 plates. Add the avocado and orange slices evenly over both plates.

2. In a small bowl, combine the vinegars, olive oil, honey, mustard, and salt and pepper and whisk. Taste, and add more salt and pepper if desired. Drizzle over the greens and top each plate with the feta cheese.

Sweet Cicely

Myrrhis odorata

Apiaceae

Sweet cicely is a perennial native to the central and southern areas of Europe and is found growing in many parts of Europe. It is also known as cow chervil, great chervil, sweet fern, and smoother cicely. Seeds are a very bright green turning to black as they mature. Historically the uses of sweet cicely are limited but it was used as a strewing herb in churches. In medieval times the air in huge churches was less than to be desired and herbs were used to cover the musty odors.

Description—Culture—Growing

Sweet cicely is a graceful plant that is a hardy and deeply rooted perennial even in northern climates. Tiny white flowers are packed into four-inch-diameter compound umbels that bloom in early spring. Flowers are sweetly scented, attractive, lacy white clusters held on four-foot-tall stalks in late May. The foliage is soft, sweetly anise-scented, and looks somewhat like a fern. Sweet cicely prefers full to partial shade. Bees, butterflies, and hummingbirds like the plant. When the foliage yellows, cut the clump back to its base. Before fall arrives, more green leaves emerge for a late fall crop.

Propagation

In fall when the seeds mature they will drop to the ground (self-seed). The following spring seedlings will germinate and are easily transplanted as soon as they emerge. Don't wait long to move them since sweet cicely has a taproot and is difficult to transplant when the taproots are big. Be sure to add a label or stake where the seeds were sown.

Uses

The anise aroma is in the stems, leaves, and unripe seeds. Sweet cicely is a forgotten herb in the kitchen and requires creativity to use it in salads, soups, breads, and desserts. The foliage, which resembles ferns, can easily be chopped and sprinkled on salads, fruit, soups, and stews. The flavor is sweet, hence the name, sweet cicely. When the seeds are still green they are soft enough to chew and are refreshing when you are in the garden on a warm June day. You can also use sweet cicely in foliage arrangements, or the leaves may be added to fish or any dish where tarragon is added. All parts of the plant are edible and the flower buds can be used for decorative purposes. Due to its natural sweetness, it is used in rhubarb and other stewed fruit dishes to help reduce a fruit's acidity. When I harvested the leaves one time, I had far too many for a recipe. I cut up the remaining leaves, dried them on cookie sheets, and sealed them in a glass jar. The dried leaves have the same aroma and flavor as fresh ones.

Rhubarb Sweet Cicely Dessert

Moist, colorful, and tasty are the words to describe this irresistible dessert.

3 cups 1-inch pieces rhubarb

3 cups quartered strawberries

½ teaspoon cinnamon

⅓ cup all-purpose flour

½ cup finely chopped fresh sweet cicely

1 cup granulated sugar

Topping

1 cup rolled oats

1 cup all-purpose flour

1 cup packed brown sugar

¾ cup butter, melted

¼ cup finely chopped fresh lemon verbena leaves

1. Preheat the oven to 350 degrees F. Butter a 13x9x2-inch baking dish.

2. Combine the rhubarb and strawberries in a medium-sized bowl and add to the prepared baking dish. Combine the cinnamon, flour, sweet cicely, and sugar in a bowl. Sprinkle over the fruit in the baking dish. Toss to mix well.

3. For the topping, combine the rolled oats, flour, brown sugar, butter, and lemon verbena in a medium-sized bowl and spread the mixture over the top of the fruit. Gently pat the topping until it's smooth.

4. Bake 35 to 40 minutes or until it's bubbly. Let it sit for 1 hour before serving. Serve with ice cream or whipping cream.

A friend's garden near Cologne, Minnesota, is overflowing with thyme.

Thyme

Thymus spp.

Lamiacea

Thyme is native in Eurasia and is a perennial aromatic herb. There is a wide range of variation among the cultivated plants. You will find that, as with so many other plants, there are taxonomic differences of opinion among the experts, with accepted names and synonyms for the same plant making it difficult at times for the writer to decide on correct nomenclature. This situation is not uncommon with other herbs also. In regards to thyme, Mrs. M. Grieve, author of *A Modern Herbal* (1931), wrote, "The affection of bees for Thyme is well known and the fine flavour of the honey of Mount Hymettus near Athens was said to be due to the Wild Thyme with which it was covered (probably *T. vulgaris*), the honey from this spot being of such especial flavour and sweetness that in the minds and writings of the Ancients, sweetness and Thyme were indissolubly united. 'Thyme, for the time it lasteth, yieldeth most and best honie and therefor in old time was accounted chief,' says an old English writer. Large clumps of either Garden or Wild Thyme may with advantage be grown in the garden about 10 feet away from the hives."

Description—Culture—Growing

Thymus species are evergreen woody perennials, shrubs, or subshrubs with small aromatic leaves. A number of *Thymus* species are hardy in cold climates, but it is always best to check local growers' advice for hardiness. Some are grown as groundcovers, others as specimen plants, and almost always small, striking flowers will appear in the summer.

Propagation

The thymes you can grow from seed is limited. As far as I know, *T. vulgaris* is one of the few, if only, that is grown successfully from seed. Seeds are very small and do not need covering when they're sowed; just keep the top of the soil moist until the seeds germinate. Other *Thymus* species and cultivars are propagated by cuttings, usually taken in early spring. In the garden, oftentimes plants will root along a stem, which can be separated from the main plant and replanted into the garden or potted for a container. When propagating plants such as *T. x citriodorus* 'Aureus' (variegated lemon thyme) or *T.* 'Argenteus' (silver thyme), it is essential to take cuttings from the variegated stems and not the green stems in order to reproduce it as a variegated plant.

Uses

Not all thymes are used for culinary purposes, but those that are have versatile flavorful leaves that have many uses. For example, the culinary thymes can flavor beef and poultry, sauces, stuffings, stews, salad dressings, vegetables (especially carrots), and soups. French thyme, *T. vulgaris*, is an essential ingredient in dried seasoning mixes where it can be mixed with butter or olive oil and garlic, spread on a cut loaf of crusty French bread, and warmed in the oven. Add whole sprigs of thyme to a slow cooker with any meats or vegetables to add flavor to the dish.

Thymes to Grow

'FOXLEY' THYME

T. pulegioides 'Foxley'

In February 2018, several friends and I
met near San Antonio, Texas, for a winter
getaway vacation. Since we are all "herbie
friends" we visited gardens and greenhouses.
One of the greenhouses on our travels
carried a thyme named 'Foxley'. It struck me
as an unusual thyme in that it looked like a
golden variegated lemon thyme, but it had
the flavor of a French thyme. 'Foxley' forms
a clump with its small cream and green
leaves that are variegated with yellow and
white. It was developed at Foxhollow Herb
Nursery, Carshalton, Surrey, England. It was
introduced in 1977. Foxhollow Nurseries
was a wholesale nursery business for 35
years supplying plants in the southeastern
part of the United Kingdom. It grows to
about ten inches tall and is mat-forming. I
do not yet know if it is winter-hardy in my
Minnesota garden, but I will certainly know
in the spring. Even if it does not survive it is
well worth growing for its beauty and flavor.

Martina Slater's 'Foxley' Thyme

"We started our smallholding in 1982. We brought with us some plants, including broad-leaved thyme as stock (mother) plants from the herb nursery in West Sussex that I had worked at for a few months. It was a few years later that I noticed a variegated offshoot on one of the broadleaved thymes and decided it was worth propagating to see if I could start a new variety. It took six years of constantly selecting suitable material for cuttings before the plant looked how we wanted it to. Often the plants would revert to normal colouration, the markings were unattractive or they were unhealthy, and died. There were occasions when we just gave up but finally, Eureka, one plant came out as we hoped—it stayed variegated, [and] was healthy and vigorous throughout the year. To get that one plant we had done thousands of cuttings over six years to come to one that was worthwhile. We then had to name the new variety. 'Foxley' had a pleasant ring to it and there was a Foxley Lane near our nursery. It took several years for 'Foxley' thyme to become known. As we were a relatively small company we couldn't afford to advertise widely but gradually more and more British nurseries started to stock it. I would occasionally Google the name to see how popular 'Foxley' was becoming. Then one day I saw it was mentioned in the United States, later still, in many other countries. It feels wonderful to have created a plant that will live on, hopefully, long after we are gone. I always knew it would be a winner and I think 'Foxley' hasn't let us down. 'Foxley' thyme is not only very attractive, it is also a top culinary thyme with a wonderful rich flavor, producing lots of leaves and stems for drying or adding straight to stews, casseroles, stuffing, or simply rubbing on meat. Suitable for first time growers of herbs as it is very easy to grow. 'Foxley' looks amazing in the early part of the year—the young foliage is pink-tinged, making it look as if it's in flower then later in the year the flowers truly cover the plant giving a second stunning display. Suitable for a sunny position in well-drained soil, it grows better if the flowers are trimmed off after flowering to encourage more vigorous growth."

Potato Parsnip Gratin

This recipe is an ideal combination of potatoes, cream, and cheese. The beauty of this dish is that it can be assembled before company arrives, then baked as you prepare the rest of your dinner. Use sharp cheddar because the flavor is more intense.

1 cup whipping cream

1 cup milk or buttermilk

2 shallots, finely chopped (or ⅓ of a finely chopped onion)

1 clove garlic, peeled and minced

1 tablespoon fresh thyme leaves

1 teaspoon chopped fresh rosemary

1 teaspoon salt

½ teaspoon freshly ground black pepper

2 pounds Yukon Gold or russet potatoes, sliced

2 medium-sized parsnips, shredded

1 cup shredded cheddar cheese

1 cup shredded Gruyère or Emmental cheese

185

Thyme

1. Preheat the oven to 375 degrees F. Lightly oil a 9x13-inch baking dish.

2. Combine the cream, milk or buttermilk, shallots, garlic, thyme, rosemary, salt, and pepper in a medium-sized bowl. Blend well. Pour 1 cup of this mixture over the bottom of the prepared baking dish.

3. Layer one-third of the potato slices in the baking dish, pressing the potatoes into the cream mixture. Spread half of the parsnips over the potatoes. Pour ½ cup of the cream mixture over the top. Spread the cheddar cheese over the parsnips and cream.

4. Layer one-third of the potato slices over the top of the cheddar cheese. Then add the remaining parsnips. Spread the remaining one-third sliced potatoes on top. Pour the remaining cream mixture over all.

5. Spread the Gruyère or Emmental cheese evenly over the top. Cover with foil and place the baking dish on a baking sheet.

6. Bake in the preheated oven for 50 minutes. Remove the foil and bake another 15 to 20 minutes, or until the vegetables are tender when pierced with the tip of a knife and the top is crisp and golden brown. Let stand 2 to 3 minutes, or until the potatoes have absorbed the extra liquid.

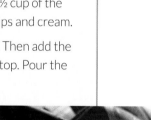

Tip: As an alternative to parsnips, wash and thinly slice 1 leek and slice 1 small onion. In place of the first layer of parsnips, spread all of the leek slices over top the potatoes, and use the onion slices in place of the second half of the parsnips.

'HALL'S WOOLLY' THYME

T. praecox subsp. *britannicus* 'Hall's Woolly'

'Hall's Woolly' thyme is a dense ground-hugging thyme whose green leaves are dotted with many small, scattered hairs on the outer edges of the leaf, giving it a silvery cast. Upon close inspection of the leaves the hairs are standing straight up. Pink flowers appear the latter part of June for up to two weeks. It is a nice filler in walkways and rock gardens. These plants can be divided the same way as 'Minor' thyme (see the following).

'LEMON FROST' THYME

T. 'Lemon Frost'

You might assume that 'Lemon Frost' implies a slight variegation in the leaf of this lemon-scented thyme—but not so. The name alludes to its pure white flowers; it looks like a white carpet when it's in full bloom, and it is very fragrant. It is a fast-growing thyme, two to three inches in height, and one that has overwintered a number of years in my garden. If you can cut enough material from this plant it has a pleasant lemon flavor but it is a short-stemmed plant and takes time to cut the foliage.

'MINOR' THYME

T. praecox subsp. *britannicus* 'Minor'

'Minor' thyme is the smallest thyme that I have grown or even seen. It is a perennial that is grown as a slow-spreading groundcover or as a filler planted between stepping stones. It forms a mat one-half to one inch tall with tiny, rounded, fuzzy, blue-green leaves. In July, clusters of tiny, rose-purple flowers appear that continue right into September. I've not found it to have any culinary purpose; besides, it's too small to harvest. You will find this plant under several names in the trade, and its cultivar name refers to its tiny leaves. When you want to increase your numbers of this plant and move it to other parts of the garden, it is easy. Just take a sharp knife and cut it like cake in a pan, into little squares, and plant these plugs where you want it to grow. There are only a few thymes you can divide this way, and it works perfectly. It needs full sun and well-drained soil. It's a plant I like to grow in fairy and rock gardens. It is even attractive to bees.

Thymus 'Minor' growing in a fairy garden makes a great addition.

RED CREEPING THYME

T. praecox subsp. *britannicus* 'Coccineus'

This vigorous creeping thyme is one to two inches tall and does well in the northern climates of the country as a hardy perennial. Red creeping thyme has tiny, glossy, dark green leaves covered with bright, light red flowers in summer. It has woody stems and somewhat tough foliage that tolerates heat and humidity well. It also will withstand light foot traffic.

Vietnamese Coriander

Persicaria odorata

Polygonaceae

Vietnamese coriander is a tropical and subtropical herb that is native to southeastern Asia. Vietnamese coriander is known by other names, and in Malaysia its name is kesom. It was introduced to the United States by immigrants from Southeast Asia as *rau ram* (often pronounced "zow-zam"), and it can easily be found in many areas of the country in farmers' markets in Asian communities. Perhaps if you despise cilantro you might like Vietnamese coriander.

Description—Culture—Growing

The aroma is similar to cilantro with a hint of lemon. Just cooking this herb will infiltrate your home with its odor. Even though you may think it is pleasing, not everyone may agree with you. It is a tender perennial in colder climates of the United States. The lanceolate leaves on a short petiole have a distinctive dark purple marking in the center of the pointed leaves. I've not seen it blooming but some state it has red flowers and yet others say, pink. The fragrance is similar to cilantro, spicy and lemony. In Vietnamese cuisine it is served raw in salads and noodle soups. Vietnamese coriander produces a pungent and warm taste in the mouth. In northern climates it grows robustly to thirty inches tall.

Propagation

It is easily propagated by root cuttings and it will even root in water—almost before your eyes. The plant stalks will also root themselves where they meet the ground line. It likes a moist site and will take some shade. Perhaps I can be happy it is not a perennial in northern climates; otherwise, it might take over my garden. To keep a fresh crop cut the plant back by one-third every three or four weeks.

Uses

The Vietnamese use herbs in cooking to finish their dishes, and this is characterized by the use of fresh herbs as an accompaniment to foods. Small bowls filled with herbs are placed on the dinner table, and guests choose the herbs they would like to flavor their individual dishes. The Vietnamese use this herb to flavor chicken and escargot (snails). When you use cilantro in cooked foods it is added near the end of cooking to avoid cooking the essential oils out of it. It is the opposite with Vietnamese coriander in that it retains its aroma and flavor throughout the cooking process; it should be added early in cooking for flavors to develop in the dish. In southern Vietnam this herb is traditionally served raw as a garnish accompanying spicy fish soups. It also goes well with meats. In Malaysia it is eaten like spinach, either raw or cooked. It is also used medicinally in Southeast Asia.

Fish Stew

This dish is such a great combination of flavors and colors! The Vietnamese coriander really adds to the flavor of the stew. The red curry paste adds a nice flavor to the soup also. Look for it in the spice section of the grocery store. Serve this stew with crusty bread to soak up all of the tasty sauce.

1½ cups seafood broth

1½ cup coconut milk

2 tablespoons red curry paste

2 coin-sized slices peeled fresh ginger

Juice of ½ lime

¼ cup finely chopped fresh Vietnamese coriander leaves (rau răm)

2 tablespoons honey

4 ounces cleaned and deveined medium shrimp, halved

4 ounces cleaned scallops, quartered

4 ounces halibut, cut into small cubes

1 cup bean sprouts

1. In a 4-quart pot, whisk the seafood broth, coconut milk, curry paste, and ginger together. Heat over high heat, stirring occasionally, until it's boiling. Add the lime juice, coriander, and honey. Reduce the heat and simmer for 10 to 12 minutes to blend flavors.

2. Remove and discard the ginger slices. Add the shrimp, scallops, and halibut and cook, stirring gently, for 4 or 5 minutes or until fish is opaque and flakes easily with a fork. Add the sprouts and cook for 1 or 2 minutes or until heated through. Serve with crusty bread.

Yerba Buena

Micromeria douglasii

Lamiaceae

Yerba buena is as well known to Californians as spring wildflowers are to people in the northern climates. This small vine grows in shaded woodland areas where it is naturally damp. It grows in warm areas such as Oregon, Washington, and British Columbia. Yerba buena was discovered by the Spaniards in San Francisco Bay on an island they later named Yerba Buena. Mary Elizabeth Parsons writes in *The Wild Flowers of California*, "Before the coming of the Mission Fathers, the Indians used this little herb, placing great faith in its medicinal virtues, so that the Padres afterward bestowed upon it the name of 'yerba buena'—'the good herb.' It is still used among our Spanish-Californians in the form of a tea, both as a pleasant beverage, and as a febrifuge. It is a remedy for indigestion and other disorders."

Description—Culture—Growing

Yerba buena is a creeping, flat vine that is a perennial in frost-free climates, spreading to two feet, with white flowers. It likes moisture and a location under a tree is a perfect setting. It's a non-aggressive, trailing plant that's easy to maintain. The stems grow across the ground and send out roots when touching the ground. It can be grown easily in containers. Dr. Arthur Tucker, Emeritus Professor and Emeritus Director, DOV, says there are at least five forms with different aromas: a spearmint-scented form, a pennyroyal-scented form, two peppermint-scented forms, and a camphor-scented form. This charming little plant is also deer resistant.

Propagation

Propagate by taking cuttings in early spring from the stock (mother) plant. But there is another method to increase plantings. As the plant grows in the garden, it sends out roots along the plant stems. These rooted cuttings can be cut from the main plant and repotted.

Uses

Its aromatic perfume is subtle. The leaves are quite fragrant and make a healthy and tasty minty tea. It has long been used by Native Americans medicinally for relief of indigestion, insomnia, colds, fevers, arthritic pain, and toothache.

A moss lined table in a garden
Atlanta, Georgia

Herb Farm near Battle Creek, Michigan

Glossary

Annual – plants that grow from seed to maturity and die in a single growing season.

Anxiolytic – herbs used to reduce anxiety.

Ayurveda – Ayurveda is a science of life (*Ayur* = life, *Veda* = science or knowledge).

Biennial – plants that live for two years, blooming and fruiting the second year.

Calyx – The sepals of a flower that form a whorl. It encloses the petals and forms a protective layer around a flower in bud.

Calyces – plural of calyx.

Carminative – herbs that can help eliminate or prevent gas from the gastrointestinal tract.

Entire – with a continuous unbroken margin.

Essential Oil – Aromatic chemical components produced by the plant.

Ethnobotany – The scientific study of the relationships that exist between plants and people.

Etymology – The origin of words and their historical development.

Eugenol – a chemical constituent of essential oils of certain plants, for example, cloves, nutmeg, cinnamon, basil, and bay leaf. Eugenol has a pleasant, spicy, clovelike aroma.

Evergreen – plants that keep green living leaves all winter.

Febrifuge – herbs used to reduce fever.

Follicle – a dry fruit that is derived from a single carpel and opens only on one side to release its seeds.

Gamma linoleic acid – a fatty substance found in various plant seed oils such as borage.

Genus – the principal category in the nomenclatural hierarchy between family and species.

Glaucous – a pale grey or bluish green appearance of the surfaces of some plants.

Herbaceous – plants that die back to the ground at the end of the growing season.

Hydrocyanic acid – the solution of hydrogen cyanide in water.

Inflorescence – a cluster of flowers on a branch or a system of branches. They are categorized generally on the basis of the timing of their flowering and by their arrangement on an axis.

Indigenous – plants that grow naturally in a particular region or environment.

Lanceolate – shaped like a lance head, much longer than wide and widest below the center.

Linalool – a component of essential oils, including orange, lavender, rose, rosewood, and coriander.

Methyl chavicol (Estragole) – a chemical constituent of essential oils of certain plants, for example, basil and tarragon. It has a sweet, anise, and spicy aroma.

Mucilage – a thick, gluey substance produced by plants. Mucilage in plants plays a role in the storage of water, food, and seed germination.

Nutlets – botanical name for seed in the mint family.

Pedicel – the stalk of a flower.

Peduncle – the stalk of an inflorescence.

Perennial – plants that live for more than two years.

Pollinators – hummingbirds, bats, bees, beetles, butterflies, and flies that carry pollen from one plant to another as they collect nectar.

Rosmarinic acid – a polyphenol derived from many common herbal plants of the Lamiaceae family: rosemary, sage, basil, marjoram, thyme, mint, lavender, perilla, and lemon balm.

Scape – a leafless flower stalk arising directly from the ground.

Serrate – toothed along the leaf margins.

Species – the category that follows genus in the nomenclatural hierarchy.

Stamen – the male component of the flower consisting of the anther and filament.

Styptic – (herb) serving to contract organic tissue.

Tender perennial – perennial plants that are not hardy in all climates.

Umbel – an inflorescence with short internodes and long pedicels.

Undulating – leaves having a wavy outline or appearance.

Bibliography

Akhila, Anand. *Essential Oil-Bearing Grasses: The Genus Cymbopogon*. Boca Raton, FL: CRC Press, 2010.

Belsinger, Susan, and Tina Marie Wilcox. "Our Favorite Oregano in the Kitchen." *The Herbarist* Vol. 70 (2004): pp. 4–10.

Biggs, Matthew, Jekka McVicar, and Bob Flowerdew. *Vegetables, Herbs, and Fruit*. Buffalo, NY: Firefly Books, 2013.

Burger, Hannah, Andreas Jurgens, Manfred Ayasse, and Steven D. Johnson. "Floral Signals and Filters in a Wasp- and a Bee-Pollinated *Gomphocarpus* Species." *Flora* Vol. 232 (2017): pp. 83–91.

Carlson, Cornelia. "Cardamom – The Queen of Spices." *The Herb Companion 9*, no.2 (1997): pp. 32–38.

Clebsch, Betsy. *The New Book of Salvias*. Portland, OR: Timber Press, 2008.

Crocker, Pat. *The Herbalist's Kitchen*. New York: Sterling Epicure, 2018.

Dufresne, Richard F. *Salvia Placard Handbook*. Greensboro, NC: (self-published), 1997.

Etcheverry, Angela V., and Stefan Vogel. "Interactions Between the Asymmetrical Flower of *Cochliasanthus caraculla* (Fabaceae: Papilionoideae) with its Visitors." *Flora* Vol. 239 (2018): pp. 141–150.

Everett, Thomas H. *The New York Botanical Garden Illustrated Encyclopedia of Horticulture*. New York: Garland Publishing, 1981.

Fleisher, Alexander, and Zhenia Fleisher. "Identification of Biblical Hyssop and Origin of the Traditional Use of Oregano-Group Herbs in the Mediterranean Region." *Economic Botany* Vol. 42, no. 2 (1988): pp. 232–241.

Foster, Steven, and James Duke. *Field Guide to Medicinal Plants and Herbs of Eastern and Central North America.* 3rd ed. Boston: Houghton Mifflin Harcourt, 2014.

Greuter, Werner, and Rosa Rankin Rodriguez. "Revision of the Caribbean Endemics Currently Placed in Nashia (Verbenaceae)." *Willdenowia* Vol. 46, no. 1 (2016): pp. 5–5.

Grieve, Mrs. M. *A Modern Herbal.* New York: Hafner Publishing Co., 1931.

Harlos, Carol Ann, "Eat Your Atriplex." *The Herbarist* Vol. 73 (2007): pp. 25–27.

Hauk, Warren D. "A Review of The Genus Cydista (Bignoniaceae)." *Annals of the Missouri Botanical Garden* Vol. 84, no. 4 (1997): pp. 815–840.

Ietswaaet, J. H. *A Taxonomic Revision of the Genus Origanum (Labiatae).* Hingham, MA: Leiden University Press, 1980.

Kennedy, Diane. *From My Mexican Kitchen: Techniques and Ingredients.* New York: Clarkson Potter, 2003.

Kuebel, K. R., and Arthur Tucker. "Vietnamese Culinary Herbs in the United States." *Economic Botany* Vol. 42, no. 3 (1988): pp. 413–419.

Llamas, Kirsten Albrecht. *Tropical Flowering Plants.* Portland, OR: Timber Press, 2003.

Makri, Olga. "*Ocimum* sp. (Basil): Botany, Cultivation, Pharmaceutical Properties, and Biotechnology." *Journal of Herbs, Spices, and Medicinal Plants* Vol. 13, no. 3 (2008): pp. 123–150.

Martinez-Nataren, Daniela A., Victor Parra-Tabala, Gabriel Dzib, Violeta Acosta-Arriola, Karina A. Canul-Puc, and Luz Maria Calvo-Irabien. "Essential Oil Yield Variation Within and Among Wild Populations of Mexican Oregano (*Lippia graveolens* H.B.K.-Verbenaceae), and its Relation to Climatic and Edaphic Conditions." *Journal of Essential Oil Bearing Plants* Vol. 15, no. 4 (2012): pp. 589–601.

McLean, Teresa. *Medieval English Gardens*. New York: Viking Press, 1981.

Meyers, Michele. "Basil, An Herb Society of America Guide." *Herb Society of America* (2003).

Moldenke, Harold N. "Notes on the Genus *Nashia*." *Phytologia* Vol. 46 (1980): pp. 172–180.

Parsons, Mary Elizabeth. *The Wild Flowers of California, Their Names, Haunts, and Habits*. New York: Dover Publications, 1966.

Pham, Mai, and Ben Fink. *The Flavors of Asia*. Buffalo, NY: Firefly Books, 2009.

Popenoe, John. "Moujean Tea." *Fairchild Tropical Garden Bulletin* Vol. 18, no. 1 (1973): pp. 12–14.

Puttock, Christopher. "The Morphology and Generic Position of Australian Kailarsenia (Rubiaceae: Gardenieae." *Nordic Journal of Botany* Vol. 4, no. 5 (1994): pp. 515–526.

Pyne, Robert, Josh Honig, Jennifer Vaiciuinas, Adolfina Koroch, Christian Wyenandt, Stacy Bonos, and James Simon. "A First Linkage Map and Downy Mildew Resistance QTL Discovery for Sweet Basil (*Ocimum basilicum*) Facilitated by Double Digestion Restriction Site Associated DNA Sequencing (ddRADseq)." PLoS ONE 12, no. 9 (2017): 1-23, doi:10.1371/0184319.

Ravindran, P. N., and K. J. Madhusoodanan. *Cardamom: The Genus Elettaria*. Boca Raton, FL: CRC Press, 2002.

Rivera, Diego, Conchita Obon, and Francisco Cano. "The Botany, History and Traditional Uses of Three-Lobed Sage (*Salvia fruticosa* Miller) (Labiatae)." *Economic Botany* Vol. 48, no. 2 (1994): pp. 190–195.

Rollins, Elizabeth. "*Origanum*: Beauty of the Mountains." *Pacific Horticulture* (Summer 1991): pp. 19–26.

Sawyer, William H., Jr. "Medicinal Uses of Plants by Native Inaguans." *The Scientific Monthly* Vol. 80, no. 6 (1955): pp. 371–376.

Singh, Narendra, Yamuna Hoette, and Ralph Miller. *Tulsi, Mother Medicine of Nature.* Lucknow, India: International Institute of Herbal Medicine, 2002.

Small, Ernest. *Culinary Herbs, 2nd Edition*. Ottawa, Ontario: NRC, CA, 2006.

Small, Ernest. *Top 100 Exotic Food Plants*. Boca Raton, FL: CRC Press, 2012.

Talbert, Rexford. "Amaracus." *The Herbarist* Vol. 70 (2004): pp. 11–13.

Tucker, Arthur, M. Maciarello, and L. M. Libbey. "Essential Oil of *Satureja viminea* L. (Lamiaceae)." *Essential Oil Research* Vol. 12, no. 3 (2000): pp. 283–284.

Tucker, Arthur, and Thomas DeBaggio. *The Encyclopedia of Herbs*. Portland, OR: Timber Press, 2009.

Tyagi, Rishi K. "Micropropagation and Slow Growth Conservation of Cardamom." *In Vitro Cellular & Development Biology* Vol. 45 (2009): pp. 721–729.

Underhill, Linda L., and Jeanne Nakjavani. "Lovage." *The Herb Companion* Vol. 5, no. 1 (1992): pp. 56–59.

Upson, Tim, and Susyn Andrews. *The Genus Lavandula*. Portland, OR: Timber Press, 2004.

Van der Veen, Marijke. "The Roman and Islamic Spice Trade: New Archaeological Evidence." *Journal of Ethnopharmacology* 167 (2015): pp. 54–63.

Van Pelt Wilson, Helen. *The Joy of Geraniums*. NY: M. Barrows & Co., Inc., 1965.

Weaver, Richard E., Jr., E. and Patti J. Anderson. "Jasmines, A Diversity of Plants with Fragrant Flowers." *Florida Department of Agriculture and Consumer Services*, Botany Circular no. 38 (2012): pp. 1–6.

Yinger, Barry R. "Lurid Purple Giants." *The Washington Park Arboretum Bulletin* 56, no. 4 (1993-94): pp. 5–7.

Yinger, Barry R. "New Perennials from East Asia." *Plants & Gardens* 47, no. 3 (1991): pp. 66–69.

Sources

Accents for Home and Garden
Peppers Greenhouse
13034 Cedar Creek Road
Milton, DE 19968
accentsforhomeandgarden.com

Andersen Horticultural Library
Minnesota Landscape Arboretum
3675 Arboretum Drive
Chaska, MN 55318
lib.umn.edu/ahl

Baker Creek Heirloom Seeds
2278 Baker Creek Road
Mansfield, MO 65704
rareseeds.com

Blooming Junction
35105 NW Zion Church Road
Cornelius, OR 97113
bloomingjunction.com
Does not ship plants

Digging Dog
31101 Middle Ridge Road
Albion, CA 95410
diggingdog.com

Fresh Start Herbs
1477 East Hastings Lake Road
Jonesville, MI 49250
freshstartherbs.org

Herb Society of America
9019 Kirtland Chardon Road
Kirtland, OH 44094
herbsociety.org

International Herb Association
P.O. Box 5667
Jacksonville, FL 32247-5667
iherb.org/

Johnny's Seeds
955 Benton Avenue
Winslow, ME 04901
johnnyseeds.com

Joyful Butterfly
1006 Hopewell Church Road
Blackstock, SC 29014
joyfulbutterfly.com

Kathleen Gips
Flora's Dictionary: The Victorian Language of Herbs and Flowers
152 South Main Street
Chagrin Falls, OH 44022
440-247-5039
$16.95, plus $4.99 shipping

Kelley and Kelley Nursery
2325 South Watertown Road
Long Lake, MN 55356
kelleyandkelleynursery.com
Does not ship plants

Kristen Macauley
Kristen Emma Photography
kristenEmma.com

Mai Pham, Cookbook Author and Chef/
Owner
Lemon Grass and Star Ginger Restaurants
Sacramento CA 95825
lemongrassrestaurant.com

Mountain Valley Growers
38325 Pepperweed Road
Squaw Valley, CA 93675
mountainvalleygrowers.com

Pat Crocker
536 Mill Street
Neustadt, Ontario
N0G 2M0
patcrocker.com

Richters Herbs
357 Highway 47
Goodwood, ON L0C 1A0
Canada
richters.com
richters.com/SeedZoo

Sandy Mush Herb Nursery
316 Surrett Cove Road
Leicester, NC 28748
sandymushherbs.com

Strictly Medicinal Seeds
P.O. Box 299
Williams, OR 97544
strictlymedicinalseeds.com

The Shop Monticello
Thomas Jefferson Foundation, Inc.
P.O. Box 318
Charlottesville, VA 22902
monticelloshop.org

The Spice House
1031 3rd Street
North Old World
Milwaukee WI 53203
thespicehouse.com

Well-Sweep Herb Farm
205 Mount Bethel Road
Port Murray, NJ 07865
wellsweep.com

Index

Credits

Photo

Photographs and recipes © Theresa Mieseler, except for the following used with permission

Bea Osborn: 217, author photo

Kathleen Gips: 168-169, Tussie Mussie, steps 1, 2, 3

Kristen Macauley: 25, *O. selloi*; 42, *Elettaria cardamomum*; 69, *Hibiscus sabdariffa*; 91, *Lavandula dentata*; 91, *Lavandula multifida*; 138, *O. syriacum* subsp. *syriacum*; 146, *Stachytarpheta jamaicensis*; 147, *S. mutabilis*; 148, *Rosmarinus officinalis* 'Shady Acres'; 159, *S. microphylla* 'Wild Watermelon'

Martina Slater: 183, *Thymus* 'Foxley' flower and leaves

Pat Crocker: 185, Potato Parsnip Gratin; 46, mortar and pestle with cardamom seeds; 48, Indian Garam Masala Spice Blend; 45, cardamom seed

Patty Kenny: 88-90, lavender wands

Rodo and Nikos Vasilaki: 133, Mountains in Crete

Shutterstock: © chuyuss: 117, Potted mint; ©Dar1930: 130, *Origanum* on cutting board; ©Josiah True: 140, Papalo at farmers' market; ©kc.bangkaew: 70, Hibiscus flower; © Linnette Engler: 145, Butterfly eating nectar from a porterweed flower; © Chamille White: 203, Old books and herbs; © Shaiith: 204, Potted herbs

Steve Taylor: 186, *Thymus* 'Lemon Frost'

Susan Betz: 105, Lovely Lemon Potpourri, Lovely lemon potpourri ingredients

Tim McCormack: 156, *Salvia clevelandii* flower, ©Tim McCormack, https://creativecommons.org/licenses/by-sa/3.0/

Recipes

Pat Crocker: 185, Potato Parsnip Gratin; 47, Indian Garam Masala; 48, Garam Masala Chicken; page, 143, Herbed Tapenade

Susan Belsinger: 28, Pasta with Summer Tomatoes and Basil. *Basil, An Herb Lover's Guide*

Mai Pham: 98, Lemongrass Lemonade. *The Best of Vietnamese & Thai Cooking*

Marge Clark: 29, Herbed Olive Oil Dip for Bread; 153, Grilled Rosemary Chicken; 102, Lemon Verbena Pound Cake, *The Best of Thymes*

A friend's garden near Jonesville, Michigan

About the Author

Theresa Mieseler has been growing, teaching, lecturing, and writing about herbs for over forty years. Theresa and Jim Mieseler founded Shady Acres Herb Farm and operated it for nearly forty years. She is a member and past vice president of the International Herb Association. As a life member of the Herb Society of America, she has served as the Botany and Horticulture chairperson. Theresa is honored to have been the recipient of the Nancy Putnam Howard Award for Excellence in Horticulture from the Herb Society of America in 2010. Theresa's career in horticulture began in 1969 at the Minnesota Landscape Arboretum and continued until 1991. She lives and gardens in rural Chaska, Minnesota, with her husband, Jim. In 1991 Theresa introduced 'Shady Acres' rosemary as a new cultivar.

Visit www.shadyacres.com to learn more about Theresa Mieseler and her programs.

Notes

Notes

Notes